US AIR FORCE HISTORICAL STUDY NO. 88

THE EMPLOYMENT OF STRATEGIC BOMBERS IN A TACTICAL ROLE

1941 – 1951

USAF HISTORICAL DIVISION
RESEARCH STUDIES INSTITUTE
AIR UNIVERSITY
1953

THE EMPLOYMENT OF STRATEGIC BOMBERS IN A TACTICAL ROLE

1941 - 1951

U. S. Air Force Historical Study No. 88

THE EMPLOYMENT OF STRATEGIC BOMBERS IN A TACTICAL ROLE

1941 - 1951

USAF Historical Division
Research Studies Institute
Air University
April 1954

FOREWORD

This monograph reviews the tactical employment of strategic bombers during World War II and the first 18 months of the Korean conflict. Emphasis is placed on the development of employment doctrine both before and during the period 1941-1951 and on the effects of theater conditions on conformity to official doctrine. The subject covered here is related to several other histories prepared by the USAF Historical Division: Air Historical Study No. 6, The Development of the Heavy Bomber, 1918-1944; AHS-70, Tactical Operations of the Eighth Air Force, 6 June 1944 to 8 May 1945; AHS-71, United States Air Force Operations in the Korean Conflict, 25 June-1 November 1950; AHS-89, The Development of Air Doctrine in the Army Air Arm, 1917-1941; and a draft Air Historical Study, Close Air Support Operations in the War Against Japan. The present study was written by Robert W. Ackerman, Associate Professor of English, Stanford University, Stanford, California.

Like other Historical Division studies, this history is subject to revision, and additional information or suggested corrections will be welcomed.

CONTENTS

		Page
I	INTRODUCTION	1
II	EMPLOYMENT DOCTRINE: 1918-1951	9
	The Interbellum Period: 1918-1939	10
	World War II and Korea: 1939-1951	19
	Strategic and Tactical Targets	35
III	THE MEDITERRANEAN THEATER	39
	The African Campaign: 2 June 1942-13 May 1943	39
	The Italian Campaign: 3 September 1942-2 May 1945	49
IV	THE EUROPEAN THEATER	73
V	THE PACIFIC AND ASIATIC THEATERS	98
	NOPAC: Eleventh Air Force	100
	CENPAC: Seventh Air Force	104
	SOPAC and SJPA: Thirteenth Air Force	108
	SJPA: Fifth Air Force	111
	CBI: Tenth and Fourteenth Air Forces	113
	Twentieth Air Force	119
VI	THE KOREAN CONFLICT: 1950-1951	124
	Phase I: 25 June-30 September 1950	127
	Phases II-V: 1 October 1950-31 December 1951	135
VII	CONCLUSION	149
	FOOTNOTES	156
	INDEX	176

Chapter I
INTRODUCTION

On 25 March 1918 the Germans, having routed the British Fifth Army in Picardy, were striking the Third Army front with seemingly irresistible force when they were subjected to an air assault of unprecedented strength and effectiveness. Not only were the advancing waves of German troops strafed by the fighter planes of the period--the Sopwith Camels and Dolphins, Bristol Fighters, and Wolsey Vipers--but all available bombardment aircraft were diverted from their normal tasks and sent out to scour the battlefield at minimum altitude. Several day bomber squadrons flying DH-4's and at least three squadrons of night bombing FE-2B's participated in close-support action along with two squadrons of the Royal Navy's big Handley-Pages with their four machine guns and great load of 25-pound bombs. The air arm was accorded no small share of the credit for stopping the dangerous offensive, but these laurels were won only at great expense.[1]

Twenty-six years later, in February 1944, when the vital Allied beachhead at Anzio was under the severest attack, the VI Corps of Fifth Army called for all-out air assistance. The response of the Fifteenth Air Force was spectacular. On 17 February numerous heavy bomber sorties were flown in support of ground troops. This force alone dropped 653 tons of fragmentation bombs on enemy guns, troops, and transportation, thus supplementing the strenuous activities of the medium, light, and fighter-bombers in the battle zone. At night RAF Wellingtons continued the attack.

On 2 March heavies participated in a renewed assault on front-line areas, and that night the Wellingtons patrolled all roads leading to the beachhead. The diversion of the bombers from their normal strategic targets was at once recognized as a powerful contribution to the ultimate success of the beachhead operation.[2] This was but one of many occasions during World War II when the heavies functioned as tactical aircraft.

More recently, in the first weeks of the Korean conflict, unorthodox, close-support employment of strategic bombers was almost an everyday occurrence. On 16 July 1950 eight B-29's of the FEAF Bomber Command attacked a concentration of six North Korean tanks at a road junction, as well as a number of other targets clearly tactical in nature.[3] Thereafter the B-29's contributed mightily to the tactical campaign. It is even reported that some strafing missions were flown, varying from treetop level to an altitude of 3,000 feet,[4] but most of the B-29 support missions involved precision bombing from 15,000 feet or higher of bridges, lines of communications, and materiel concentrations near the front lines. Such use of B-29's in Korea was, however, officially regarded as having been dictated by special circumstances--in particular, the lack of light bombers. It was also clearly recognized that the B-29's could continue in a ground-support role, as they did throughout 1951 and later, only because of the overwhelming air superiority, especially over the battle area, maintained by United Nations forces.[5]

. . . .

In the several combat operations cited above, aircraft designed primarily for strategic bombardment were used in a tactical role because the critical state of the ground battle demanded that all available force be applied directly against front-line enemy troops. Later in Korea, B-29's continued to be used against tactical targets even when no emergency existed, largely because all profitable strategic targets appeared to have been neutralized. But initially in Korea, as in Picardy in 1918 and at Anzio in 1944, the strategic bombers were thrown against tactical targets because of the precarious position of the ground troops.

The terms "strategic" and "tactical" require careful definition. Though a full discussion is reserved for Chapter II, the ambiguity of their meanings and the resulting possibility for confusion may be noted here. Whereas strikes at those elements of the enemy's industrial system affecting his capacity to sustain his war effort are obviously strategic, and the bombing of front-line positions are just as clearly tactical, there remain many targets which are not so readily classified. For example, the cutting of rear lines of communications might hamper the enemy's efforts to move troops and supplies up to the line of battle and would thus be reported as tactical. But the same operation might also prevent the transportation of raw materials to armament plants, in which event it could also be considered strategic.[6] Further, the examples with which this chapter begins suggest that there are several kinds of tactical missions. Strikes at enemy troop concentrations in the front lines—close support—and interdiction of communications in the vicinity of the battle area—usually referred to as isolation of the battlefield—are the two types most usually recognized.[7] Sometimes, however, one finds the phrase "indirect air support" used to describe quasi-tactical air action against approaches to a battle area, such as land and sea communications, ports, and base installations.[8]

Another source of confusion is due to the frequent application of the term "strategic" to certain bombardment types of aircraft, as in the title of this study. The expression "strategic bomber," however, is regarded as informal or unofficial usage, despite the frequency of its occurrence. The standard classifications of bombardment types are "heavy," "medium," and "light," although the B-29 was at first designated a "very heavy bomber." Throughout World War II, the heavy bombers---the B-17 and B-24---and the very heavy bomber---the B-29---were, with little danger of ambiguity, called strategic bombers, since except under the special conditions prevailing in the Pacific theaters they were normally reserved for long-range missions against the sources of the enemy's war potential. Postwar shifts in the classification of military aircraft, however, led to confusion. Although the B-29 was reduced to the status of a medium bomber, in the Korean conflict it was nevertheless used as a strategic bomber and was often so called.[9] Again, especially after the adoption of a functional organization by the air forces in northwest Africa in 1943, the expression "strategic air force" was commonly applied to the bomber command, whose mission was long-range strategic assault, and the medium groups and air support units came to be called "the tactical air force."[10] During World War II the Eighth Air Force in the European Theater of Operations and the Fifteenth in Italy were both primarily strategic air forces. But to add to the confusion, for a short time early in their development, such air forces, especially the Eighth, comprised not only the standard heavy bombers with their fighter groups and photo-reconnaissance wings, but some groups of medium bombers as well. And the Ninth Air Force, although organized for tactical operations, often sent its mediums out to bomb industrial and other strategic objectives in conjunction with the Eighth Air Force heavies.[11]

The term "strategic," then, whether applied to targets, to types of bombardment aircraft, or to a force of long-range bombers in a theater of operations, is subject to varying interpretations. In the present study, however, the expression "strategic bomber" is consistently used to refer to the B-17, B-24, and B-29 only, since all pertinent combat operations, World War II and Korean, employed one or another of these aircraft. A "strategic air force" is referred to only where no ambiguity is likely.

Ever since the close of World War I, the air arm has insisted that aircraft designed expressly for long-range strategic bombing could not be regarded as efficient weapons for use over the battle area in lieu of tactical aircraft and, therefore, that they should not lightly be diverted to tactical missions. Among the many prodigious technological advances in aircraft development since 1918, the specialization of combat types has been especially striking. The differences between fighters and the heavier bombers in size, speed, maneuverability, and other features became increasingly pronounced. The fighters of 1918 were only slightly faster than the largest bombers, but the speed of the World War II P-51H exceeded by more than 100 miles per hour that of the B-29. Equipment peculiar to the fighters of World War II included special armor protection for the pilot, rocket-firing mechanisms, and even cannon; the heavy bombers, in addition to a 10-man crew trained almost exclusively for high-altitude operations, carried complex navigational and bombing devices. Apart from the obvious consideration that the long-range, high-altitude characteristics of the heavy bombers would normally be wasted in tactical missions, the most compelling reasons for reserving the heavies for strategic purposes were these: 1) their low flexibility would make them far less capable than tactical aircraft of effective evasive action over a battle area heavily defended by enemy antiaircraft artillery and fighter planes; and 2) their great size and relatively slow speed made them far better targets for enemy gunners.[12]

The present study aims to determine to what extent the tactical use of strategic bombers in combat operations both in World War II and the Korean war through 1951 conformed to official Air Force employment doctrine. To this end, Air Force doctrine on the differentiation between strategic and tactical air power, and on the conditions under which strategic bombers may be diverted to tactical objectives is examined. There follows a summary of the principal instances, as reported in the combat histories of all theaters of World War II and of the conflict in Korea through 31 December 1951, in which strategic bombers--the B-17, B-24, and B-29--were used in situations which would be defined as tactical in standard Air Force doctrine and which would thus normally call for the use only of fighter-bombers or medium bombers. These activities were, for the most part, close-support and interdiction missions. Only clear-cut combat activities are here accepted as tactical, to the exclusion of such operations as leaflet-dropping and trucking flights.[13] The degree of success achieved in each operation is discussed whenever evaluations by responsible observers are available.

The reader, however, is warned not to expect decisive evaluations of the effectiveness of all bomber operations which are here analyzed. To the extent to which adequate evaluations are not available, the general conclusions of the present study must be regarded as tentative. As will be seen, a satisfactory assessment of the contributions made by B-17's, B-24's, and B-29's to any tactical situation in which they were called upon to participate was, more often than not, exceedingly difficult. Even when expert target teams were able to examine the target within a reasonable time after the bombing, they sometimes could not arrive at any sound conclusions about the credit due the strategic bombers. The principal difficulty was that many of the tactical objectives had been hit not only by the strategic bombers but also by medium and light bombers and even by friendly artillery and naval gunfire, so that apportionment of credit was quite impossible.[14] No doubt it is for this reason, among others, that we find military men expressing contradictory views on the value of such employment of the heavy bombers. Gen. Omar N. Bradley, for example, speaks out vigorously against close support by the heavies. He even quotes General Eisenhower as being of like mind in his account of the action at Saint-Lô, in which strategic bombers bombed short on the 30th Infantry Division, a tragedy which cost the life of General McNair.[15] On the other hand, Marshal of the RAF Sir Arthur T. Harris, referring to several World War II engagements, states just as forcefully his conviction that strategic bombers proved themselves extremely capable in close-support operations.[16]

The existence in military circles of so wide a range of opinion is in itself, perhaps, sufficient justification of the present study.

Chapter II

EMPLOYMENT DOCTRINE: 1918-1951

Two concepts in Air Force doctrine have a particularly important bearing on the present study. These concepts are, first, the recognition of strategic bombing as a highly significant element of air power; and, second, the justification of occasional diversions of strategic bombers to tactical missions. The intimate relationship existing between the two is obvious: until the existence of strategic bombing came to be clearly recognized, there could scarcely be any question as to the propriety of the non-strategic use of strategic bombers. The second concept thus emerged as a corollary to the first.

Although the strategic role which would be played by heavy bombers in World War II, especially in Europe, was readily apparent shortly after the opening of hostilities, the concept of strategic air warfare was not completely formulated as part of American employment doctrine until the publication of Field Manual 100-20 in mid-1943. In the same directive is to be found for the first time a realistic approach to the problem of transferring heavy bombers from strategic to tactical missions. A full understanding of both these concepts, nevertheless, is dependent on a knowledge of their evolution in earlier statements of Air Corps doctrine. Hence, the present history of employment policy begins with a rapid summary of the prewar period rather than with the field manual of 1943.

Again, since doctrinal developments cannot readily be discussed apart from the conditions which usually gave rise to them, especially in those cases where doctrines were formulated under the stress of war, a number of allusions to combat operations are included in this chapter. The capabilities and limitations of some of the aircraft which the framers of Air Corps doctrine had in mind are also noted.

The Interbellum Period: 1918-1939

Before the end of World War I the chief combat roles which aircraft were to play were fairly well delineated if not fully tested. The earliest capacity in which World War I aircraft served was observation and reconnaissance, but the counter-air function soon came to assume great importance as squadrons of pursuit planes armed with machine guns engaged in the first great air battles. Ground-support aviation also came to be used with skill and success. The prime necessity of massing attack planes over a particular sector threatened by enemy air rather than spreading a thin umbrella of defense over the entire front was a lesson quickly learned and brilliantly applied by Brig. Gen. William Mitchell. Unhappily, it was a lesson that needed to be relearned in north Africa 24 years later. Strategic bombing, however, was not destined to receive the test of battle during World War I. It is true that the British did become cognizant of the great advantages to be reaped in bombing German industrial centers and, to this end, in 1918 organized the Independent Force as a component of the RAF, the successor to the Royal Flying Corps. But the 10 night-bomber squadrons of the Independent Force were only beginning their work when the armistice was signed.[1]

The realization in the United States that strategic bombing had particular relevance to the defense of the American continent fortunately came early enough to make possible the development of the B-17 and the other long-range bombers of World War II. A more imaginative leadership, supported by a more generous Congress, might have foreseen the need for long-range fighters as well, but, as it was, the United States fought a great part of the war in both the European and Pacific theaters without proper escort protection for bombing missions. The years of peace were also marked by the evolution of the specifically American concept of high-level precision bombing, a concept which led to the perfecting of elaborate computing bombsights. Because the interest here is entirely in tactical operations, however, to enter upon a systematic account of strategic bombing during World War II or of the controversial value of high-level precision bombing is unnecessary. It suffices to remind the reader that, so far as the European war is concerned, the strongest claims made for strategic bombing were spectacularly vindicated. In the words of the Overall Report of the United States Strategic Bombing Survey:[2]

> Allied air power /that is, the Combined Bomber Offensive of 1943-1944/ was decisive in the war in western Europe. . . . Its powers and superiority made possible the success of the invasion. It brought the economy which sustained the enemy's armed forces to virtual collapse, although the full weight of this collapse had not reached the enemy's front lines when they were overrun by Allied forces. . . . the indications are convincing that they would have had to cease fighting—any effective fighting—within a few months. Germany was mortally wounded.

The airmen who were able to envisage such tremendous benefits as these were most anxious to preserve the integrity of their sustained strategic offensive and to avoid diverting their bombers to tactical targets.

In the interval between the two wars, the significance of strategic air power came to be a central issue in the long struggle of the American air arm for proper recognition and autonomy. The limited, subordinate role allotted to military aviation in the 1920's is well illustrated by a field regulation of 1923. Here, the mission assigned to each of the different classes of aviation then recognized was described. The mission of pursuit, said to be the most vital element of the air service, was first to secure and maintain air superiority, thus permitting the execution of the other missions, whereas attack aviation was designed to deliver blows to enemy ground troops. The task of bombardment aircraft was somewhat more fully explained:[3]

> The mission of bombardment aviation is the bombardment of ground objectives. It operates particularly against hostile territory beyond the effective range of artillery. It carries out bombing operations both by day and night. Objectives of particular importance to bombardment aviation are those vital to the functioning of the enemy's line of communications and supply (railways, railroad stations, important bridges, supply depots, airdromes, etc.).

Just as reconnaissance and attack aviation were merely adjuncts to ground operations, so bombardment aviation had no independent mission. The targets stipulated above were more nearly tactical than strategic. As viewed by this directive, bombers were merely a means of extending the range of artillery.

Elsewhere, the same regulation recognized that each of the several combat functions was best performed by the "types of airplanes, armament, and other equipment adapted to its mission." At the same time, however, the need for a degree of flexibility was emphasized:[4]

> The several classes of aviation are not restricted in their employment to the missions to which they are specialized. In varying degrees, all classes are qualified to execute the various aviation missions; their employment is governed by the relative importance of the several missions, the strength of the available air forces, and the limitations of the types of airplanes employed by each class.

The principle of flexibility of employment, although somewhat at variance with the clear need for more specialization of military aircraft types, was, as will be seen, never completely lost sight of in air doctrine.

A training regulation of January 1926 appeared to strike a new note in its treatment of the function of air power:[5]

> The mission of the Air Service is to assist the ground forces to gain strategical and tactical successes by destroying enemy aviation, attacking enemy ground forces and other enemy objectives on land or sea, and in conjunction with other agencies to protect ground forces from hostile aerial observation and attack.

Later, the regulation spoke briefly about coastal bomber patrols and the bombing of capital ships. There was also a paragraph devoted to "strategical bombardment," which was described as flying deep into hostile territory "with the objective of destroying sources of military supply, main lines of communication, and military industrial centers." The employment of air strength might weaken the enemy both through damaging military production and transportation and also by causing discontent and alarm. "In addition," the paragraph concluded, "it may compel him to withdraw a portion of his pursuit and antiaircraft from the combat zone."[6]

The terse reference to the destruction of sources of supply and of industrial centers suggests, at first glance, an enlarged view of the potentialities of air power, but immediately thereafter the regulation stated carefully that such operations were conceived of as a direct furtherance of ground strategy—again, as extending the effective range of artillery. This impression is reinforced by the statement that strategic bombardment was a means of forcing a diversion of enemy air power and antiaircraft batteries from the battle area. One must conclude that the authors did not realize the independent nature of true strategic bombing, nor did the Air Corps Act of a few months later (2 July 1926) reflect any essential change in official thought on this subject.[7]

So imprecise and inadequate a conception of strategic bombing as noted above could not have been gratifying to those air officers who, two years earlier, had committed to writing a quite different formulation. In an Air Service Tactical School manual used as early as 1924, air activities having "an immediate effect on the operation of the ground forces" were defined as tactical operations, whereas strategic missions were those "planned in furtherance of the national aim." As such, the strategic bombing force should be at the disposal, not of divisional or other subordinate commanders, but of GHQ.[8] Chiefly because they viewed strategic air as capable of striking a powerful blow at an enemy quite independently of the ground forces, influential air officers found themselves far from agreement with the General Staff as to the proper status of the air arm.

The cleavage between the War Department and air officers continued, as is shown by a survey of the texts issued by the Tactical School at Langley Field. An Air Corps Tactical School text entitled The Air Force, dated 1931, dealt expressly with the functions of an air task force rather than with the GHQ Air Force, which had not yet come into existence. Nevertheless, the authors made some general observations on the objectives of air power. These they classified as political, strategic, and tactical. The objectives then termed political, such as attacks on enemy cities for the purpose of damaging civilian morale, would now be considered strategic. Strategic objectives were defined as the key points in the enemy's supply, reinforcement, and evacuation systems. The authors believed that sustained bombing of such targets should comprise a large proportion of the activities of an air task force. Tactical missions would include direct support of ground troops, blocking avenues of escape of a defeated foe, and destroying supplies and munitions. Some of these targets could also, under certain circumstances, be termed strategic, but as was frankly admitted, "there is no clear line of demarcation between the two terms."[9]

Some space in the manual was given over to warnings against the "tendency to employ one class of aviation for purposes for which another class exists." It was observed that each class of military airplane was a highly specialized instrument which would "rapidly lose efficiency if diverted to other tasks." Even though the "proper province of bombardment overlaps that of attack to a limited extent" because the weapon of both was the bomb, the commander was warned to "guard against the error of employing his attack and bombardment indiscriminately . . . ."[10] The proponents of strategic air power were likely to stress the desirability of limiting each combat type to its proper mission.

Another 1931 textbook of the Tactical School, Bombardment Aviation, further emphasized the principle of the proper employment of each of the classes of combat aircraft:[11]

> Bombardment aviation is essentially a weapon of GHQ. Its potential power of destruction indicates clearly that it should normally be used only against targets which are not capable of destruction by the fire of attack aviation or artillery or which are outside the radius of action or range of these arms. . . . No matter what the strength of the bombardment component, it is improbable that a sufficient number of bombardment units will be available to strike all these objectives. There will probably be certain vital objectives comparatively limited in number which, if destroyed, will contribute most to the success of the combined arms of the Nation.

This highly condensed statement was, in some respects, reminiscent of the manual of 1924 already quoted. In speaking of strategic bombardment as contributing "to the success of the combined arms of the Nation," the writers echoed the national aim theory and stressed their belief that strategic air power must be independent of tactical demands. Again, just as in the 1924 manual, this broad concept of the contribution of strategic bombing was used as an argument for reposing control of the bomber force in GHQ rather than parceling it out to ground commanders. The passage further indicated that some thought had been given the problem of distinguishing tactical from strategic targets and of selecting proper strategic targets. In general, the rather rough distinction here set up between the two categories of objectives was one or range. Everything beyond the range of attack planes would seem *ipso facto* to have been considered a strategic target, a point of view which World War II experience, especially in the Pacific theaters, tended to confirm. Elsewhere, the old World War I doctrine that the light bombers would normally operate by day and the heavy strategic bombers by night was stated with approval.[12]

It is of perhaps more than parenthetical interest to note here what bombardment airplanes the air officers had in mind when setting forth these views. In 1931 the backbone of the Air Corps bomber fleet was the B-3A, the Keystone Panther, although the Curtiss Condor was also still in service.[13] The fabric-covered B-3A, with its open gunners' positions, service ceiling of 12,000 feet, high speed of about 100 miles per hour, and a maximum range of 510 miles with a normal bomb load of 1,995 pounds, was, within a period of 3 years, to be superseded by the slightly smaller Martin B-10, an all-metal monoplane with a 21,000-foot ceiling, speed of 207 miles per hour, and a maximum range of 507 miles with a normal bomb load of 2,260 pounds. The B-17, with much more impressive speed and bomb capacity and vastly extended range, was not produced until 1935.[14] These later airplanes, complex and costly as they were, would be even less expendable in short-range tactical operations than the earlier bombers.

Although the views of the Air Corps on strategic bombing were by no means fully acceptable to the War Department, they appear to have had some slight influence on the 1935 revision of the doctrinal manual, The Employment of the Air Forces of the Army. Because the regulation of 1935 was still in force when the European war broke out four years later, it merits detailed examination.

The general mission of air power was defined as comprising "the air operations required for carrying out the Army mission."[15] Although this statement would seem to reflect the same attitude toward the subservience of the air arm as the 1926 regulation, we find, in the account of the responsibilities of the GHQ Air Force, that some provision was made for a strategic bombing force. The GHQ Air Force was to include "all air combat units and auxiliaries thereto organized and trained as one force capable of operating in close cooperation with the ground forces, or independent thereof." In peacetime, the entire air combat force would operate under the Chief of Staff, but in time of war this control would pass to the commander in chief of the field forces, who was to see that all air activities accorded with the "Army Strategical Plan covering a specific situation and with the strategical and tactical plans promulgated to govern specific operations."[16]

Air activities in "immediate support of the ground forces," or tactical operations, were rather carefully treated. Prior to battle, a four-phase program was recommended: 1) interdiction of enemy air reconnaissance and enemy air attacks; 2) air reconnaissance to provide security, or to obtain information; 3) air attacks against enemy communications and movements; 4) air attacks against enemy concentrations, moving columns, and ammunition dumps.[17] Strategic targets, or "those air operations beyond the sphere of influence of the ground forces" were listed, apparently in order of priority: 1) air forces; 2) combatant surface and submarine vessels; 3) munitions factories, refineries, and fuel-storage plants; 4) factories producing aircraft and aircraft equipment; 5) critical points on lines of communications; 6) power plants, power lines, and other utilities; 7) troop cantonments and troop concentrations.[18]

The principal advance one notes in Training Regulation 440-15 for 1935 is that in the outline of the responsibilities of the GHQ Air Force the separate tactical and strategic missions of air power was recognized.

On the other hand, the classification of counter-air operations as jointly strategic and tactical and the reference to "the Army Strategical Plan covering a given situation" suggest that the members of the General Staff had not allowed the promise of air power to alter in any fundamental way their conception of modern warfare.[19] It is impossible to believe that the framers of this regulation could have acquiesced in the prophetic dictum appearing in the 1931 manual, The Air Force: "With the exception of operations against an enemy air force /here regarded as a tactical responsibility/, a large proportion of the operations of an air force will be against strategical objectives."[20]

When World War II opened with the German invasion of Poland, Training Regulation 440-15 was the official statement of employment doctrine.[21] It is probably fortunate that it was not subjected to an immediate test in combat, because it established no clear-cut policy for the control of strategic air power, and it was no more effective as a guide for tactical operations, since it lacked any close consideration of the fundamental problem of air-ground cooperation. One may say, then, that at the time war broke out strategic bombing as a highly significant aspect of air power had barely achieved recognition in official doctrine, and no realistic body of principles governing the use of this weapon had as yet been worked out. Certainly, no procedures were outlined for such exigencies as the transfer of strategic bombers to tactical operations.

World War II and Korea: 1939-1951

The combat lessons of the early months of World War II were not lost on air officers in the United States, but some time elapsed before these lessons came to be clearly reflected in alterations and elaborations of existing doctrine. Field Manual 1-5 of 1940, superseding Training Regulation 440-15, for example, did not offer a great deal that was new. It did, however, provide for a striking force and a support force within the GHQ Air Force. Moreover, it set forth specifically the mission of strategic air operations. Such operations were to be undertaken by bombardment aviation in order to nullify the enemy's war effort or to defeat important elements of the hostile military force.[22] The furtherance of the Army's strategic plan was not mentioned as the proper mission of bombardment. And there was a passing recognition that bombers might on occasion function as tactical aircraft, even though procedures for such tactical employment were not formulated: "The tactical employment of bombardment aviation depends to a large extent on the situation and upon the nature of the surface objectives whose attack or destruction will contribute materially to the accomplishment of the general plan."[23] Perhaps Field Manual 1-5 was significant principally because it distinguished between the support and the strategic responsibilities of the GHQ Air Force more categorically than had earlier directives.

In two directives issued in 1941 we find ample evidence of the impact of the European war on Air Corps thinking. The German use of aviation, and especially of the dive bomber, in the _Blitzkrieg_ in Poland, the Low Countries, and France, seems to have exerted a powerful influence on the field tests conducted by the GHQ Air Force in response to a War Department directive in the first half of 1941 and on the doctrine derived from those tests. The purpose of the test was to develop appropriate doctrine for the use of the light bomber in close support, and Training Circular 52, published in August, was particularly concerned with depicting the results. This training directive provided no evidence, however, that the use of heavy bombers in close support was clearly visualized at this time, even though the general principle was laid down that "all classes of aviation may be used to support ground forces."[24] The kinds of support missions suitable for bombers were listed as follows:[25]

1) Reconnaissance bombardment: developing and attacking targets that impede the advance of the supported unit.

2) Attack on defensive organizations: air attacks on field fortifications and defensive organizations in the path of the supported ground forces, when it was not practicable to employ other means.

3) Attacks on enemy reserves and reinforcements: striking hostile forces moving toward the operations area of the supported unit.

4) Attacks on hostile mechanized forces: attacks designed to forestall counteroffensives by such enemy units.

5) Support of friendly armored or motorized forces: continuing support of such ground units after the success of the initial attack for the purpose of detecting and attacking hostile resistance.

6) Support of parachute troops and air infantry in the air and on the ground.

Although it was conceded that close-support objectives on the immediate front or flanks of the supported unit were often transitory targets of opportunity which the aircrews themselves would select and bomb, normal target selection was left in unmistakable terms to the ground commander alone. Such targets included troop concentrations, bridges, motor columns, and minor field fortifications such as pillboxes. Against these, it was recommended that dive bombers be used. Other targets farther from the front lines could include command posts, lines of communications, ammunition dumps, bivouacs, and airdromes, against which what were referred to as "horizontal bombers" would presumably be effective. Targets not suitable for aerial bombardment were defined as small objectives very near bodies of friendly troops and targets which were within the range of ground weapons.[26] Beyond this, attention was given to the establishment of advanced air-support command posts at or near the command post of the supported ground unit. Responsibility for coordinating combined air-ground operations fell to the ground commander, although the exact method of air attack to be followed in a given situation was to be determined by the air commander.[27]

Training Circular 52, then, was a milestone in the development of realistic ground-support tactics and procedures. Its concern quite naturally was with tactical aircraft. Such references as it contained to "horizontal bombers" may be construed to include heavy bombers, but the use of such an imprecise term strongly suggests that the authors of the directive had not contemplated the possibility of throwing strategic aircraft into close-support activities.

The next directive, Training Circular 70, was published a few days after Pearl Harbor. Strategic air operations were here defined as those capable of exerting air power to a distance greater than the operating radius of hostile bombardment. Strategic activities, a function of the Air Force Combat Command, successor to the GHQ Air Force, could be controlled and employed directly by the Chief of Staff, by a task force commander, or by a theater commander. The designation of systems of strategic objectives, such as the oil or the electric power industries of the hostile nation, was a duty of the Chief of Staff or of the theater or task force commanders, but specific targets within these systems were to be selected by air commanders alone. These provisions represented progress toward recognition of the mission of strategic bombing and the protection of that mission.

At the same time, the possibility that a critical ground situation might create an overriding demand for tactical support was also acknowledged. The directive stipulated that when such close support of ground forces was needed,[28]

> all types of combat aviation, heavy, medium, and light bombardment, pursuit and observation aviation must be ready to accomplish this mission. Each type of aircraft will be employed against the targets most suitable to its particular characteristics. Air support is assigned by the theater commander to the major elements of attacking ground forces.

In preparation for just such emergencies, it was ordered that each class or category of aviation personnel be trained in at least two kinds of employment. Although the primary emphasis in the training of bomber crews was to be placed on the "will and ability to reach and destroy objectives at the maximum radius of action," it was considered equally important that they be taught the methods best calculated to provide direct support to ground troops.[29]

In April 1942 both of the above training circulars were superseded by Field Manual 31-35, Aviation in Support of Ground Forces. No sweeping change in the principles set forth in the training circulars appeared here, the chief difference being that more detailed attention was given the problem of control over air-support operations. The manual provided for an air force which would normally include an air support command, the commander of which was to serve as an adviser to the army, theater, or task force commander in all matters pertaining to air. There was to be no direct assignment of air power to ground commanders, although air support elements might be attached to subordinate ground units.[30] Air support targets were discussed in much the same terms as in the earlier directives, but more emphasis was placed on the possibility of danger to friendly troops in close-support bombardment. It was admitted that no satisfactory method of "insuring immunity to troops" had been developed, but careful target selection, proper briefing of aircrews, and adequate methods of marking the bomb line were recommended as means of reducing the danger to a minimum.[31]

The training circulars of 1941 and Field Manual 31-35 together defined the close-support doctrine which governed the AAF's participation in World War II. Further changes were proposed during the summer of 1942 as a result of new tests, but these were not accepted.[32]

The employment doctrines discussed above grew largely out of vicarious experience and maneuvers. Except for early activities in the Pacific, where combat conditions differed radically from those encountered elsewhere, the first sustained contact American airmen had with the enemy was in Africa. American air units first joined the RAF in the Egyptian delta and the Middle East in June 1942, the month of the disheartening Knightsbridge disaster and the loss of Tobruk to Marshal

Rommel. In November 1942 the Twelfth Air Force moved into northwest Africa in support of the Allied landings, and there followed many months of indecisive action in the course of which the earlier conception of air support, involving the lavish use of all available fighter aircraft as a defensive umbrella over the ground troops, was completely discredited. There were also examples of a wholly unwise selection of targets for bombardment by ground officers. The air support command doctrine outlined in Field Manual 31-35, had it been formulated earlier, might well have forestalled some of these abuses. As it was, however, an air support command, as called for in the field manual, was not established until mid-January 1943, and it was then so soon supplanted in a basic reorganization of the Northwest African Air Forces that it cannot be said to have received a fair test.[33]

The great benefits arising from the reorganization of all Allied air forces in Africa after 18 February 1943 have been frequently discussed. The new plan, principally British in conception, was designed to secure flexibility, mobility, and concentration of air power. Speaking in very general terms, these aims were accomplished through the establishment of a centralized control of all air support, and, indeed, of all air power in the Mediterranean area, in the Northwest African Tactical Air Force. Further, all air umbrellas not specifically authorized by the tactical air force commander were banned, and joint air-ground headquarters were set up in which air and ground commanders enjoyed equal status in decisions on the use of the air weapons.[34]

Subsequent Allied successes in northwest Africa could in large measure be so clearly attributed to the reorganization that the lessons of this campaign were soon translated into new doctrine. The earliest formulation, however, was not an official manual or regulation but a group of informally written pamphlets prepared for the guidance of theater and overseas air force commanders. These publications, entitled collectively "The Air Force in Theaters of Operations: Organization and Functions," may well have been written in response to a letter of March 1943 to the Director of Bombardment, Headquarters, AAF, from Col. Charles G. Williamson of the Directorate of Bombardment. Colonel Williamson emphasized that the "lack of an authoritative and concise statement of AAF doctrine and employment policies" was responsible for many failures and for conditions that were "almost chaotic" in the air operations he had observed in combat zones. The employment of heavy bombers against unworthy targets was, in his opinion, one of the worst offenses.[35] Most of the pertinent material contained in these pamphlets, which were published in May 1943, were better stated in the field manual of July 1943, to be discussed next. It should here be mentioned, however, that one of the pamphlets dwelt on the difficulty of distinguishing between targets appropriate for medium and heavy bombers. After acknowledging that it was no more feasible to distinguish sharply such targets than to separate exactly various classes of artillery targets, the pamphlet stated that[36]

> the distance to a target and the target's importance to the enemy's total effort might be stated as the prime factors in determining which type of bomber is the most logical for a mission. Although the heavy bomber can, if necessary, attack

at short range, it is the only airplane, in fact the only weapon, which can consistently attack in vital and distant rearward areas. Therefore, it would seem logical to reserve it mostly for such missions, leaving more advanced enemy parts to be hit by possibly less valuable and shorter-ranged weapons, or even by more valuable weapons designed for the purpose but which cannot normally do the long range job.

Here, in succinct form, was given what is perhaps the best argument for protecting strategic bombers from inordinate tactical demands.

Field Manual 100-20, Command and Employment of Air Power, published 21 July 1943, was the official enunciation of the doctrine learned in the bitter northwest African experience, and it remained the bible for tactical operations throughout the rest of World War II. This directive, largely the work of Col. Morton H. McKinnon, assistant commandant of the AAF School of Applied Tactics, began by announcing the coequal status of land and air power: "neither is an auxiliary of the other."[37] The first requirement for the success of any major land operation, and the first priority for air power, was the winning of air superiority. Counter-air activity, however, was acknowledged to be of continuing importance throughout any given campaign. The theater commander, who would exercise control of the ground forces through the ground commander and of the air force through the air commander, was expressly forbidden to attach air elements to ground units except when such units were isolated or acting separately.[38] These general provisions were clearly designed to prevent such misuse of air power as had occurred in Africa.

The normal theater air force, as outlined in the manual, included a strategic air force, a tactical air force, an air defense command, and an air service command. The general aim of the strategic air force was defined as the defeat of the enemy nation—the same mission as that of the ground forces, but one which it would pursue independently through the destruction of "important establishments in the economic system of the hostile country." Here at last, it would seem, was an acknowledgment in plain language of the necessarily independent nature of strategic bombing. Plans for strategic operations were to be formulated by the War Department General Staff, although the selection of strategic targets became the task of the theater commander acting through his air force commander. The strategic air force normally would have heavy bombardment as its mainstay and also fighter and photographic aviation. The fighter planes would furnish escort for the bombers and would also defend the bomber bases from attack.[39]

The tactical air force, consisting of reconnaissance aviation, light and medium bombardment units, and fighter aircraft was to serve both the ground forces and the theater as a whole. The mission of the tactical air force was described as falling into three phases:

First priority: Air superiority. To be gained by attacks against enemy aircraft in the air and on the ground, and against enemy installations.

Second priority: Isolation of the battlefield. To be gained by the disruption of hostile lines of communications, the destruction of supply dumps, and attacks on enemy troop concentrations.

Third priority: Close support of ground troops. To be accomplished by destroying selected objectives in the battle area. In order to maintain close teamwork, the command posts of the tactical air force and of the ground force concerned should be adjacent or common. Phase lines or bomb lines were to be carefully established and rigidly respected.[40]

Furthermore, Field Manual 100-20 was explicit on the transfer of strategic bombers to tactical missions. In the course of describing the proper activities of the strategic force, it was noted that "although normally employed against objectives listed above, when the action is vital and decisive, the strategic air force may be joined with the tactical air force and assigned tactical air force objectives."[41] This principle was extended somewhat in a later paragraph: "In a particularly opportune situation (offensive) or a critical situation (defensive), a part or a whole of the strategic air force may be diverted to tactical air force missions."[42] Although nowhere directly stated, the clear intention of the directive was that strategic aircraft, when participating in a tactical program, should pass under the control of the joint air-ground headquarters—that is, of the tactical air force.

The field manual did not spell out such procedural details as the channels which requests for strategic air should follow. In actual practice air and ground personnel were usually able to work out these matters smoothly through close cooperation. Combined tactical and strategic operations were successfully arranged at Kasserine Pass, Salerno, Cassino, and elsewhere.

The new version of Field Manual 31-35, appearing in August 1946, introduced no changes in the basic principles, although some of the procedures developed during the war for requesting and controlling tactical missions were here put into writing.[43] A proposed revision of this manual dated March 1949 offered further refinements, such as an attempt to distinguish "support, close air" from "support, general air." The former would consist of attacks on targets "so close to friendly forces as to require detailed integration with the fire and movements of these forces," whereas general air support would comprise operations in the enemy rear areas beyond the range of friendly artillery.[44]

A statement of the lessons of air support learned in the European war was also written by FM Bernard L. Montgomery in December 1944. After pointing out that all modern military operations were in fact combined army/air operations, Montgomery discussed at length the problems of planning and control of air support. Negotiation rather than command, he believed, was the key to working out effective plans for the air phase of a combined action. The principle of adjacent headquarters was not in itself sufficient if a true meeting of minds on the part of army and air officers were not effected. Only after priorities had been arranged at the highest echelon could air power be allocated to particular sectors of the front. Otherwise, small packets of air power should never be placed under army formation commanders because each air detachment would then be set to work on a limited plan of action. Montgomery further cautioned army commanders that, whenever air support was essential to winning a battle, they had to be prepared to await favorable weather for the air strikes. Moreover, he pointed out that when a bomb line was too far ahead of friendly troops, the army forces were likely to lose faith in their air support.[45]

The still current Joint Training Directive for Air-Ground Operations, prepared by the Army Field Forces and the Tactical Air Command in 1950, is the most inclusive statement of doctrine to be issued to date. An entire chapter entitled "Strategic Bombardment Aviation in Close Support of Ground Forces," provides a full statement of principles and procedures involved in the diversion of bombers to a tactical role. The chapter opens with a warning:[46]

> The effect of strategic air warfare must not be compromised by dissipating the strategic air effort on relatively minor targets. It is essential, therefore, that strategic air units not be diverted to a large tactical operation, unless it appears certain that the effect of large concentrations of munitions from the air on the enemy ground forces will materially affect the outcome of the ground battle.

The support action which could best be carried out by strategic bombers was said to consist normally of carpet bombing or area attacks, which would require careful coordination with ground forces to insure their safety and an immediate follow-up. The ground situation should be sufficiently stable to permit the mounting of such a mission, which would necessarily be "pre-planned" rather than "immediate" or spontaneous.[47] The processing of requests for strategic participation was outlined as follows: any request by a ground commander for a bombardment mission was to be forwarded through Army channels to the tactical air commander who would honor it within the limits of his available forces as long as the targets in question were, in his opinion, suitable. If, however, the tactical air commander decided that the targets were better suited to strategic bombers, he was to transmit the request to the theater air commander who had to decide, in the light of the general military situation, whether to order strategic bombers to fly the mission in question. Once assigned to a tactical mission, the strategic bombers would function under the operational control of the tactical air command. It was hoped that the close liaison made possible by joint air-ground headquarters should greatly accelerate the procedure just outlined. The strategic air commander should be given advance notice of an impending call on his resources whenever possible through a tactical air force representative.[48]

The preliminary planning for close support by strategic aircraft, it was stipulated, had to begin at the tactical air force/army group level. Full target details had to be secured and all necessary coordination with the ground forces completed. In particular, the ground forces were made responsible for marking the bomb line with fluorescent panels, barrage balloons, antiaircraft shell bursts, or electronic devices.[49]

Requests for strategic aviation in other tactical operations such as an interdiction program would normally be initiated by the tactical air commander and be processed as described above. The several types of interdiction recognized in the directive included bombing lines of communications or troop movements and three kinds of reconnaissance: photographic, visual, and electronic.[150] Strategic bombers might be asked to assist in all these capacities, and, as will be seen, actually did so in Korea.

The foregoing review of air force employment policies has traced the slow development of official recognition of strategic bombing as a highly significant means of striking directly at vital points of the enemy's productive system and thus at his capacity to wage war. Although officers of the air arm had been conscious in varying degrees of the great potentialities of strategic operations since the establishment within the RAF of the Independent Force, and although they sought to pass on their vision of modern warfare through the medium of textbooks used in the Tactical School in the early 1930's, their influence was not sufficient to alter the convition of the General Staff that air power was a feeble weapon when functioning independently of the ground forces. Even in the 1935 directive, in which such genuinely strategic objectives as aircraft factories and power plants were listed as proper targets for the bombers of the GHQ Air Force, the controlling view was that the general mission of air power was to assist in carrying out the Army plan. A clear acknowledgment that the strategic air forces had the same general aim as the ground forces—the defeat of the enemy nation, but that it would pursue this aim by entirely different means and therefore independently of the Army—did not appear as official doctrine until July 1943, when World War II was more than half over. The next step, once the equal status of air and ground had won acceptance, was autonomy for the air arm.

Employment policy was governed almost from the beginning by two seemingly antithetical principles. One was that for each of the several military missions of air power—reconnaissance, pursuit, bombardment, and the like, there should be available an aircraft especially developed, so far as technical possibilities permitted, for the efficient performance of that mission. Normally, each type was to be limited to its special task. At the same time, it was allowed that emergencies might arise which would interfere with the exact matching of combat missions with available types of aircraft. Perhaps the earliest clear recognition that the concept of multiple employment for combat types had a significant bearing on training appeared in Training Circular 70 in 1941. Here, as already noted, it was stipulated that each type of aviation be trained in at least two kinds of employment. The secondary function envisaged for heavy bomber crews, one gathers, was close-support activities. But after the United States entered battle in December 1941, the pressure of events made impossible such prolongation of bomber-crew training[51]--a fact of considerable importance to the present study.

Up to the appearance of Training Circular 70, highly generalized statements of the old principle of flexibility constituted the only evidence that employment other than strategic was as much as contemplated for the recently developed heavy bombers. There was little need to work out careful plans for the transfer of heavy bombardment to such tasks before the distinctive mission and, therefore, the separate organization of strategic air power came fully to be recognized. Transfer and control procedures were first outlined in the field manuals of 1943 and 1946, and they received much more detailed treatment in the training directive of 1950. In the following chapters, which study combat operations, the effectiveness of these policies and measures will be, so far as the evidence permits, discussed.

Strategic and Tactical Targets

Reference has already been made to the lack of any definite line of demarcation between tactical and strategic targets. A further comment on target classification is advisable before describing the combat operations of World War II and in Korea.

In one of the earlier allusions to strategic targets, appearing in Training Regulation 440-15 for 1926, the sources of military supply, military industrial centers, and transportation systems were listed as strategic objectives.[52] In the 1935 revision of this directive, in which the list was extended, combatant surface vessels, submarines, munitions factories, critical points on lines of communications, power plants, and troop cantonments were also included.[53] Training Circular 70, (1941), stated that strategic targets would include specifically the oil and electric power industries of the hostile nation,[54] whereas Field Manual 100-20, (1943) indicated more broadly that these targets were the important establishments in the enemy's economic system and also the vital communications centers.[55]

In all these directives there was essential agreement that war production plants and the major power installations of the enemy, along with communications centers, such as railroad yards, inland canals, and seaports, constituted the ideal objectives of the strategic air force. It was possible to regard the bombing of aircraft factories not merely as a strategic program but also as a contribution to the destruction of the enemy's current air strength--the first obligation of the tactical air force. But, at least in theory, the line drawn in the directives between strategic and tactical targets would seem to be clear-cut and unmistakable. Tactical aircraft were limited to the three-phase mission of gaining air superiority, isolating the battlefield, and providing close support to ground troops. Strategic aircraft would be occupied exclusively with industrial and power plants and great communications centers, except when called on rare occasions to aid the tactical air force, when they would function as tactical bombers.

Yet, in both World War II and the Korean conflict, many bomber missions were flown against targets which, although considered strategic in the sense that they were assigned directly to the strategic air force, were quite clearly second-phase tactical objectives. Most of these targets were on lines of communications, particularly railroads, but they were by no means restricted to the great communications centers which, according to the directives, were proper strategic targets.

And even the bombing of carefully selected communications centers during World War II proved to have tactical as well as strategic implications. Nowhere were the dual benefits of communications bombardment better illustrated than in the Eighth Air Force operations over occupied Europe during 1944. During that period, the tremendous total of 90,060 tons of bombs were dropped on railroad marshalling yards, and, in addition, 18,104 tons fell on bridges and 8,091 on naval facilities and inland canals. The railroad yards absorbed more bombs than any other single class of targets hit by the strategic air force in England, receiving 22 per cent of the total tonnage expended by the Eighth Air Force during 1944.[56] The consequences of this massive, concentrated assault on communications were described as follows by the United States Strategic Bombing Survey:[57]

On the whole, it might be said that by the close of 1944 air attacks upon the transportation system, although they had not seriously reduced the ability of the Army to originate tactical moves in volume, had imposed serious delays upon such operations and often prevented units from reaching desired destinations. Moreover, they had reduced the available capacity for economic traffic in Germany to a point which could not hope to sustain, over any period of time, a high level of war production. The loss of transportation facilities completely disorganized the flow of basic raw materials, components, and semi-finished materials, and even the distribution of finished products. Under these conditions orderly production was no longer possible.

In March 1945, when in the interests of isolating the battle areas transportation was made the first priority for all classes of aircraft, more attention came to be paid to such chokepoints as railroad and highway bridges and tunnels and to movements of troops and supplies.[58] The classic example of tactical interdiction by a strategic air force, however, was Operation STRANGLE, conducted in part by the Fifteenth Air Force in central and northern Italy, which is discussed below.*

Thus air attacks on communications, even when initiated for strategic purposes, yielded obvious tactical benefits whenever the enemy's tactical movements depended upon the communications thus damaged. Furthermore, intensive line-of-communications programs primarily for the tactical purpose of isolating the enemy ground forces from sources of supply may be and have been assigned to strategic bombers, largely because of considerations of range and sometimes the nature of the targets to be destroyed. That the proper classification of such dual-purpose objectives presents a problem was recognized as early as 1931 by the author of a Tactical School manual which stated that between tactical and strategic objectives "there is no

---

*See p. 64.

clear line of demarcation."[59] A 1949 proposal for the revision of Field Manual 31-35 appeared to make an effort to facilitate such classification. For example, it was provided that the extent of the battlefield, within which all tactical operations including air would take place, would be defined by the ground commander. Outside this defined area, all operations of whatever kind would presumably be termed strategic.[60]

In the absence of such arbitrary designations of strategic and tactical areas, there is no sure guide for the classification of communications targets. It is possible, of course, to acknowledge the frequent ambiguity by calling all communications targets either "quasi-tactical" or "quasi-strategic." Yet, to avoid such vague terminology is of more than academic importance. Apart from large, widespread objectives like railroad yards and seaports, communications targets generally consisted of bridges often located in difficult mountainous terrain, tunnel mouths, small ships, and other pinpoints for which strategic bombers were by no means suited and yet which they were often sent out to bomb during World War II. As the historian of the Fifteenth Air Force observed, both in the planning of missions and in evaluating its own record of efficiency, a strategic air force necessarily had to take account of the fact that small communications targets are more properly tactical than strategic.[61]

The combat experience discussed in the chapters which follow, therefore, includes not only the missions in which strategic airplanes worked with the tactical air force in close support of ground troops and in short-range interdiction, but also certain representative long-range operations, which, like STRANGLE, required that strategic bombers be sent against objectives generally considered better suited to smaller tactical aircraft.

AHS-88

Chapter III

THE MEDITERRANEAN THEATER

As used here, the term "Mediterranean theater" embraces World War II operations by air forces of the United States in northwest Africa, Italy, southern France, and the Balkan Peninsula. American air participation in the African campaign began on a very small scale in June 1942. An imposing array of strength was built up in this theater by the end of 1943, however, and the weight of these forces had contributed much to the surrender of Axis troops in Africa on 13 May 1943 and to subsequent successes in the Mediterranean area. The assault on Sicily was preceded by the seizure of the island of Pantelleria, which succumbed to a tremendous air and naval bombardment on 11 June 1943. In turn, the invasion of Italy followed hard on the heels of the conquest of Sicily, the reduction of which required the full effort of the British Eighth and the American Seventh Armies during the period 10 July to 17 August. The stubbornly-fought Italian campaign began with the British landing (BAYTOWN) at Reggio on 3 September 1943 and lasted until 2 May 1945, anticipating V-E Day by less than a week. The heavily air-supported landing in the Toulon area of southern France (ANVIL, later DRAGOON) took place on 15 August 1944. Starting in April 1944, Balkan rail targets were bombed to provide strategic aid to the Russians and, as will be shown, some tactical air support was given the Rumanians a few months later.

The African Campaign: 2 June 1942-13 May 1943

It must be admitted that no very satisfactory analysis of the tactical use of strategic bombers in Africa can be presented here. There are several examples of this employment of B-17's and B-24's to be found in the history of the African campaign: the AAF Evaluation Board in its review of operations in the Mediterranean theater spoke of five such instances. But the board also discovered that lack of detailed information rendered impossible any sound estimate of the effectiveness of the heavy bombers on these occasions.¹ To be sure, more data than were utilized in the evaluation board's reports are now available, yet this additional information by no means takes the place of official assessments by qualified experts, such as were at hand for many of the combat actions in Italy and elsewhere. Here, largely in order to illustrate the kind of situation which called for the tactical use of heavy bombers in Africa, two combat actions are briefly described: the battlefield and line-of-communications strikes by RAF Wellingtons and U.S. heavies at El Alamein, and the bombing of enemy troop concentrations by AAF strategic bombers at the Kasserine Pass.

A short account of the disposition of American air power in Africa is necessary to understand the significance of these combat operations. Although American aid, in the form of aircraft and a small repair depot at Gura, Eritrea, was benefitting the hard-pressed British well before the end of 1941, active participation did not begin until more than six months after Pearl Harbor, and even then the first assignment of elements of the American air arm came about almost by accident. A detachment of 23 B-24's under the command of Col. Harry A. Halverson, which was en route to Chinese bases for the bombing of Tokyo, was held in the Middle

East upon landing there on 2 June 1942. The worsening situation in Africa and the realization that the supplying of B-24 bases in China would be exceedingly difficult led to this change in plans, and thereafter the Halverson Detachment functioned as a strategic unit in Egypt and the Mediterranean area. On 12 June, 13 of Halverson's planes bombed the Ploesti refineries, the first truly strategic mission flown by American crews in World War II. A few days later, the B-24's afforded protection to a British convoy threatened by the Italian navy. They seem not to have served in any tactical capacity, however, in the severe British reverses at Knightsbridge and Tobruk.[2]

The Halverson Detachment, or what was left of it after the Ploesti strike, was augmented on 28 June by a handful of B-17's flown into the Middle East from the Tenth Air Force in the CBI under the command of Maj. Gen. Lewis H. Brereton. The same month also saw the establishment of the United States Army Middle East Air Force (USAMEAF) with the Halverson and Brereton Detachments and newly-arrived B-24's and tactical aircraft as its basis. The American B-24's, now organized into the 1st Provisional and the 98th Bombardment Groups, functioned, along with the RAF 160 Squadron of B-24's, under American officers. On 27 November 1942 these AAF and RAF elements were designated IX Bomber Command. The harbors of Bengazi and Tobruk and Mediterranean shipping were frequently-visited targets of the bomber command during this critical phase of Allied military fortunes. At the same time, the crews of the American medium bombers and the American fighter pilots gained much valuable experience by flying with elements of the RAF under the command of the Western Desert Air Force. On 12

November 1942, USAMEAF became the Ninth Air Force, and as such continued to operate against Naples, Messina, and Palermo in Italy and Sicily as well as against African ports and shipping from bases which were moved from the Egyptian Delta and Palestine into Tunisia as the campaign progressed. The Ninth Air Force left Africa in August 1943, and the Twelfth Air Force, which had been operating chiefly in Tunisia since November of the preceding year, took over most of its units.[3]

The Twelfth Air Force had begun life as the American air component in TORCH, the Anglo-American landings on north Africa, launched 8 November 1942. Equipped and staffed largely by the Eighth Air Force, even to its commander, Maj. Gen. James H. Doolittle, the Twelfth Air Force came into Africa with the first landing parties and thereafter flew both strategic and tactical missions in the ensuing struggle for Tunisia. Since the north African landings were made at two widely separated points—Morocco and Algeria—the Twelfth split its tactical units, assigning to Algeria its fighter command and to the Casablanca area, much farther removed from the ground conflict, its air support command, including RAF elements. It will be recalled that American doctrine at this time provided for the control of air support target selection by ground officers, and it was under such control that XII Fighter Command was committed to umbrella defense tactics. The prime illustration of the unsoundness of this policy occurred on 4 December when a ground officer, despite protests by the air commander, ordered a squadron of RAF planes unescorted and by daylight to attack an Axis air base. The entire squadron of Bisleys was thereupon lost to enemy air action.[4] Such misuse of air power in northwest Africa, along with the obvious need for closer coordination between the AAF and RAF, led to functional reorganization and to the new doctrine of Field Manual 100-20, which has already been discussed. On 18 February 1943 the Northwest African Air Forces (NAAF) under the command of Maj. Gen. Carl Spaatz was activated and assigned to the Mediterranean Air Command (MAC) under ACM Sir Arthur W. Tedder. Subordinate to NAAF were the Northwest African Tactical Air Force (NATAF), concerned with ground cooperation in Tunisia, and the Northwest African Strategic Air Force (NASAF), comprising XII Bomber Command, some squadrons of RAF Wellingtons, and escort fighters. As already indicated, the Twelfth Air Force, as the principal component of NAAF, took over much of the Ninth Air Force when the latter was reorganized in August 1943.[5]

Thus, during the period of American participation in Africa, the Ninth Air Force was engaged in the eastern Mediterranean, Egypt, and Libya, largely under British direction, and the Twelfth in Algeria, Tunisia, and the western Mediterranean. Both air forces for most of this period were composite--that is, they contained medium bombardment groups for tactical work as well as B-17's and B-24's. The RAF's Wellingtons (classed as mediums) also engaged in strategic operations. Heavy bombers served in a tactical capacity during the African campaign in two major battles: El Alamein and Kasserine Pass.

El Alamein. The preliminaries to the battle of El Alamein, where the Eighth Army put an end to Axis designs on Egypt and the Suez Canal, began with a British attack on 3 July 1942. The enemy replied with a counterattack lasting from 30/31 August to 7 September; this battle, known as Alam Halfa, in which Allied air power played a part, was a

AHS-88, Chap. III

victory for the Eighth Army inasmuch as Rommel's forces wasted much strength in a fruitless effort to gain ground. The RAF Middle East Review spoke of the diversion during this engagement of Wellington bombers from their bombing of enemy airfields and of such ports as Bengazi and Tobruk to battlefield operations, in which they were joined by U.S. B-25's and P-40's. USAMEAF bombers of all categories, were reported to have dropped 868 tons of bombs on truck columns and troops in more than 3,500 sorties. Bomber losses were 7, compared with 26 losses for the German and Italian Air Forces. Simultaneously, strategic bombers successfully hit convoys in the Mediterranean. The available information, however, does not permit any assessment of the total damage done to the enemy by these attacks nor of the attrition for which the strategic bombers were responsible.[6]

The battle of El Alamein proper began late in October. On the eve of Montgomery's great assault, which commenced on 23 October, the RAF in the Middle East could muster over 800 operational aircraft including 383 bombers, and the American air force 130 aircraft, of which 46 were B-17's and B-24's. The air preparation, opening 19-20 October, resulted in some destruction of Axis aircraft, already numerically much inferior to Allied forces. After the beginning of the ground battle, many close-support missions were flown to prevent the development of effective counterattacks. The drive in the southern sector, which allowed the British to break through the enemy's defenses, marked the end of the battle and started Rommel on his four months' retreat to the Mareth line in eastern Tunisia. Masterly though his retreat was, Rommel could not avoid being cruelly harassed from the air. During the daylight hours, fighters and fighter-bombers strafed and bombed his columns, and from

6 to 8 November, 32 heavy bomber and 127 medium bomber sorties added their weight to the running attack on his troops and armor. Meanwhile, most of the heavy bombers were occupied with shipping in and near the harbor of Tobruk and with German airfields on Crete and elsewhere.[7]

Kasserine Pass. The air action which took place in connection with the American setback on 20-24 February 1943 at Kasserine Pass, in Tunisia near the Algerian border, provides the second major instance of the tactical use of strategic bombers. During the first weeks of 1943, detachments of Rommel's armor, now refitted after its great retreat and its establishment in the Mareth line, felt out in a number of minor engagements the strength of the forces converging on the Axis bridgehead from the north. Meanwhile, the XII Bomber Command continued its seaport, shipping, and airfield program, although on 11 January 1943 five B-17's were sent out to bomb--unsuccessfully, it turned out--the fortress of Gadames in Libya as an aid to Free French forces in that vicinity. By the end of January some improvements had been made in the unsatisfactory air support situation. Brig. Gen. Laurence S. Kuter became the commander of a new organization, the Allied Air Support Command, which comprised the XII Air Support Command and the RAF 242 Group. The experience level of the pilots and the number of A-20's, P-39's, and P-40's controlled by the XII Air Support Command were both at a low ebb at this critical time, but better use of air power was made possible by the changes. Yet air power was not sufficient to prevent the reverses at Faid Pass on 14 February and elsewhere which forced the Allies back on the western mountain range paralleling the Algerian border. The security of the Kasserine Pass in this range was placed in the hands of the American II Corps, which began preparing its defenses.[8]

Only three days before the enemy attack at Kasserine, AM Sir Arthur Coningham became commander of the new NATAF, the successor to Kuter's Allied Air Support Command. Coningham at once banned umbrella defense tactics and announced that his command would henceforth go on the offensive. But bad weather the next few days not only forestalled an immediate test of his policies but also allowed the Germans to establish themselves on high ground overlooking American positions. On 20 February the enemy attacked, routing the Americans and forcing the pass. All available tactical air power was at once concentrated on the roads in and near the breakthrough, and, providentially, the Axis columns seeking to exploit their success were stopped in their tracks and they began moving back into the pass on 23 February. At this point, strategic bombers were thrown into the fray, an action made possible by the reorganization of 18 February. The part played here by the heavies of NASAF was succinctly described in the RAF Middle East Review: "On 23 February 1943, the first day of the withdrawal proper, 45 U.S. Fortresses bombed Kasserine and 18 U.S. Marauders concentrated on the actual pass. Damage could not be assessed because of poor visibility."[9] The strategic bombers were used to harass the retreat and to destroy enemy armor.[10]

The occasions on which strategic aircraft engaged in close support in north Africa, then, were neither numerous nor particularly striking. The battlefield bombing at Alam Halfa, the harassment of Rommel's retreat of 6-8 November, and the bombing of the enemy near Kasserine on 23 February, in addition to the samll-scale attack by B-17's on Gadàmes to which allusion has been made, were all clearly tactical missions. The first seems to have been occasioned by the need to assist tactical air in close support during a critical battle, and the next were mounted to increase the destruction of enemy forces on or near the battlefield in what Field Manual 100-20 called "a particularly opportune (offensive) situation." The attack on Gadames would also be considered a close-support mission. In its study of these actions, however, the evaluation board stated flatly that a clear estimate of effectiveness could be established for none of them. The report recorded that 86 bombers were dispatched on close-support missions in north Africa but that not more than 75 per cent carried out effective sorties. Fifty-seven aircraft in all dropped 97 tons of bombs, chiefly in the Kasserine Pass, and of these 17 planes received battle damage.[11] No additional information has come to light to permit assessment of these support operations.

The principal targets of the heavy bombers in both the major combat areas in north Africa were not only harbors but also Axis shipping in the Mediterranean and airfields in Africa, Italy, and on such islands as Crete. Seaports, as has been observed, were considered legitimate strategic targets, but small ships would normally be considered tactical. The heavy commitment of B-17's and B-24's to antishipping and airfield strikes in Africa did not escape the attention of higher headquarters. Such "misuse" of heavy bombers was the subject of the letter of March 1943, already quoted, informing the Director of Bombardment, Headquarters, AAF about a number of missions illustrating uneconomical and unorthodox employment of heavies. These included attacks on small ships such as sailing vessels, airdromes located within the operating radius of light bombers, and even skip-bombing and strafing sorties.[12] Early in December 1942 General Spaatz had ordered that heavy bombers should thereafter concentrate on such strategic targets as seaports and marshalling yards rather than on airfields.[13] Against ports and railroad yards the B-17's of the Twelfth Air Force, sometimes joined in their strikes by B-25's and B-26's, achieved a good record.[14]

The difficulty was that north Africa by no means abounded in strategic objectives. Apart from seaports and other communications centers, which, as has been indicated, are almost always ambiguous in their classification as strategic, it was essentially one great tactical area. Aside from counter-air and close-support activities, the function of air power, like that of sea power, was to interfere constantly with Axis supply lines---to isolate the theater of war. The results of the successful bombing of Axis supply convoys off such ports as Bizerte were felt almost immediately by Rommel's front-line troops. The great contribution of the strategic air force in Africa was its vigorous participation in this campaign to deny supplies and reinforcements to the enemy. There was a rather belated attempt at a clear division of labor between the tactical and strategic air forces, the latter usually being assigned the seaports. But when distances were not too great even over these targets the strategic aircraft were sometimes joined by the mediums. It was scarcely possible to restrict the heavy bombardment groups to a program clearly defined as strategic by AAF doctrine. The only real distinction made between tactical targets and the targets assigned to strategic bombers was one of range.

In north Africa, as in other areas, the degree of economic and industrial development determined whether the kind of strategic program envisaged in AAF doctrine was possible or whether all classes of aircraft would operate essentially in a tactical capacity.

The Italian Campaign: 3 September 1943-2 May 1945

The reduction of Pantelleria (CORKSCREW) is not studied here, despite the fact that in the course of this remarkable operation strategic bombers cooperated closely with NATAF planes. On 11 June 1943, following three weeks of intensive bombing, the defenders of the island surrendered just as the first landing craft touched shore. The air phase of CORKSCREW, which isolated the battlefield by neutralizing Axis air bases on the Toe of Italy and on various islands, and softened enemy defenses and morale, must certainly be described as tactical. Yet the impossibility of determining how much of the destruction of military facilities on the island is attributable to bombs dropped by the heavies makes this example unsuited for present purposes.[15]

The conquest of Sicily (HUSKY) likewise opened with an elaborate air assault. But reduction of this bastion of Axis power, more than 200 times the size of Pantelleria, also required the best efforts of two Allied armies. Sicilian airfields ever since the beginning of the Mediterranean campaign had been visited by Allied bombers. After the fall of Pantelleria, a systematic counter-air and interdiction program was inaugurated with particular focus on the more than 30 Sicilian airfields used by the Axis, but Sardinia and southern Italy were also included. In the early days of the air assault on Sicily, Ninth Air Force heavy bombers assisted by RAF units, particularly fighters from Malta, struck airfields in eastern Sicily from their Libyan bases. The fields in western Sicily became the responsibility of NAAF, including American heavy and medium bombers. Many missions were also devoted to ports

AHS-88, Chap. III

and marshalling yards in both western Italy and Sicily with a view to restricting the flow of supplies and reinforcements. Beginning on 2 July, just eight days before the HUSKY landings in southern and southwestern Sicily, NASAF and IX Bomber Command combined to rain bombs on the Gerbini airfields in Sicily and then on bases in the Heel and on Sardinia.[16]

Immediately before the landing of the assault boats on 10 July, B-17's joined B-25's and B-26's in softening operations in the vicinity of the beaches, while P-38's flew strafing sweeps over the southeastern parts of the island. During the grim battle that ensued, interdiction and support action was carried on by NATAF against very light enemy air opposition, and the heavies were free to strike mainland seaports and other more distant targets, including Rome and even Ploesti. Nevertheless, the B-17's and B-24's occasionally rejoined the tactical air force in attacks on Messina, other stubbornly held enemy positions, and airdromes. Especially during the last days of the Sicilian campaign, which concluded on 17 August, were the B-17's active along with tactical planes in punishing day and night the enemy's retreat across the Strait of Messina.[17]

Thus, the strategic aircraft of both NASAF and IX Bomber Command functioned very often, if not principally, as a tactical weapon during the conquest of the Mediterranean islands. The many strikes at airfields were intended not only to destroy Axis aircraft but also to force the enemy to transfer his planes from the islands and even the nearby mainland bases to more remote localities from which he could not so readily interfere with Allied plans. In close harmony with the counter-air program was the interdiction of supply routes leading to the islands by the intensive bombing of harbors and other communications centers. Only these last-named targets could be called strategic.

AHS-88, Chap. III

Air power during the 20 months' campaign in Italy proper played a markedly different role. A number of hard-fought ground battles in Italy necessitated that strategic bombers fly missions in close support of ground troops. Authoritative appraisals are fortunately available for some of these bomber strikes. With the exception of the few attacks on power installations and industrial plants, strategic air power was used in Italy to effect long-range interdiction just as it had been in Africa and the Mediterranean. There are at least two reasons why a full-scale strategic program did not develop in Italy. First, the surrender of Marshal Badoglio's government to the Allies on 8 September 1943 left only a few plants in the north which continued, under German control, to turn out war materiel. And, second, the mission of the Fifteenth Air Force was to attack, not Italian targets, but Combined Bomber Offensive (CBO) objectives from bases in Italy.

In all, seven occasions on which U.S. heavy bombers flew tactical missions, mainly in close support, are examined here: 1) Salerno, 2) Anzio, 3) Cassino, 4) Operation DIADEM, 5) southern France, 6) Rumania, and 7) Bologna. These actions will be analyzed as fully as the available information permits.

Salerno. The prelude to the landing on 9 September 1943 of the American Fifth Army at Salerno on the west coast of Italy some 180 miles above Messina may be quickly described. Action against air bases, seaports, and communications lines in southern Italy had been essential to the success of both CORKSCREW and HUSKY. Hence, the opening of the direct assault on Hitler's _Festung Europa_ signified no fundamental redirection of effort. On 3 September, scarcely more than two weeks after the expulsion of the Germans from Sicily, the British launched their amphibious invasion across the Strait of Messina (BAYTOWN). Much of the air preparation for BAYTOWN had already been achieved as a part of the counter-air and shipping program in support of CORKSCREW and HUSKY. But airdromes were hit again and again up to 28 August, whereupon the bombers began their effort to cut all communications leading to the landing beaches. During the assault itself, the two British divisions received support from the Desert Air Force, aided by other NATAF units. Thereafter, air support became the responsibility of the Desert Air Force alone.[18]

The initial preparation for AVALANCHE, the American landing at Salerno, was merely an extension of the air preliminaries for BAYTOWN. But the next stages of air activities at Salerno were rendered difficult by the fact that fighter planes flying escort or covering the invasion itself had to work at the extreme limit of their radius of action. The role of NASAF until just prior to BAYTOWN was to hit airfields and communications above the ankle of the Italian boot; the Ninth Air Force was assigned similar targets in the Heel; and NATAF the Toe. NASAF concentrated particularly on the bases grouped around Foggia, although some tons of bombs, such as in an attack on Pisa, fell on gasworks, aircraft factories, and other strategic objectives. After BAYTOWN was under way, the Axis airfields within fighter range of Salerno absorbed punishment from the heavies and mediums, and, on the night of 8 September, the communications centers of Battipaglia and Eboli were hit. The AVALANCHE landings on 9 September were covered by XII Air Support Command, which thereafter took up the task of cooperation with the Fifth Army.[19] NASAF, the whole effort of which was assigned to protection of the landing, went to work on the communications leading to the beachhead perimeter, although some heavies continued the intensive program of airfield bombing. The enemy, fully cognizant of Allied plans at Salerno, offered strong opposition almost from the start. The Americans succeeded, however, in extending their beachhead, although they were unable to seize and hold an airfield from which fighter planes could operate at short range against the enemy. Soon it became clear that, in spite of all efforts at interdiction, more enemy troops were moving into the Salerno area, and the German attack that developed during 12 to 14 September against a weak sector of the American line came perilously near cutting through to the beach.[20]

The situation was a desperate one, and the means adopted for coping with it, so far as the use of air power is concerned, are of interest here. Since 9 September, NASAF had been working with NATAF in a strong effort to isolate the beachhead. Tactical had assumed responsibility for communications to the south and Strategic for the northern highways, road junctions, bridges, and railroads. In these activities, the heavies as well as medium and fighter-bombers participated. On 12 September the heavies and mediums bombed points like Mignano and Castelnuovo, located approximately 60 miles from the battle front, some 56 B-17 missions being flown that day. On the 13th, communications centers much closer to Salerno, such as Torre del Greco, Pompei, and Torre Annunziata, were battered. But on the 14th, when the German thrust seemed on the point of reaching the beach and slicing the American line in two, all available aircraft, including the heavies, were sent over the battlefield to render direct support to the ground troops. During this day and the next, heavy bombers alone flew 1,025 effective sorties, dropping 2,638 tons of bombs in the vicinity of Battipaglia, Eboli, and on roads directly in front of friendly troops.[21] Roads and railways took the bulk of this tonnage, only one attack having been aimed against forward gun positions and enemy troops. Unfortunately, the results of this particular close-support mission by heavies could not be determined to the full satisfaction of the evaluation board, nor do available studies by German officers throw light on the matter. One German general has observed, however, that the Allies ought to have achieved more by their attacks in the forward areas, especially against road traffic.[22] Nevertheless, it seems clear that through their participation in battle-area bombing, the crews of the heavy bombers could claim a fair share of the credit for stopping the Germans by 15 September.[23] A broad assessment of the part air power played in the critical days at Salerno was given by Gen. Harold L. Alexander:[24]

> The tremendous air attacks added greatly to the morale of the ground and naval forces, and, in addition, have inflicted on the enemy heavy losses in men and equipment. They have seriously interfered with his movements, interrupted his communications and prevented his concentration of the necessary forces to launch large-scale attacks.

As the American Fifth Army pushed slowly out of its hard-won Salerno beachhead toward a junction with the British Eighth, and the combined Allied forces commenced their drive up the Italian Boot, NASAF began a program of hitting important communications just north of Rome in an effort to head off the withdrawing Germans. At this time an important organizational change took place. By order of the Joint Chiefs of Staff (JCS) the Fifteenth Air Force was activated on 1 November 1943 under the command of General Doolittle; the Fifteenth was to serve as a strategic weapon designed to strike targets in Austria and southern Germany from Italian bases, thus assisting the Eighth Air Force in the long-planned Combined Bomber Offensive. The Fifteenth took over as its nucleus the six heavy bombardment groups belonging to the Twelfth Air Force, together with long-range fighter groups, thereby reducing the Twelfth to a tactical air force. Within the next two months, six groups of B-24's also joined the Fifteenth, and its bombers were moved from Tunisia to airfields in the vicinity of Foggia.[25]

Anzio. By the end of 1943 the Allies bogged down along a line running diagonally across Italy less than 50 miles above Naples. Operation SHINGLE, the amphibious landing at Anzio some 60 miles further up the west coast of Italy, was designed to end this stalemate and clear the road to Rome. Although the landings proceeded on schedule on 22 January 1944 and the Allied forces were able to establish themselves on a beachhead some seven miles in depth, subsequent reverses in late February necessitated the use in close support of all available aircraft, including heavy bombers. A second emergency on 2 March again sent strategic planes over the battle area. Both actions are described below.

First, however, the role of the U.S. strategic air force--that is, the Fifteenth--previous to and during the first stages of the invasion must be briefly outlined. After its activation, the Fifteenth continued on an augmented scale the work of the XII Bomber Command, which it superseded. Specifically, the air force was ordered to interrupt enemy transport north of a line reaching across Italy from Civitavecchia through Ancona. On 24 December 1943 appeared a new directive which confined transportation strikes to certain important railroad marshalling and repair yards extending from Foligno on the Civitavecchia-Ancona line to Turin and Voghera in the far northwest of Italy. Such blows, insofar as they hampered rail movements of troops and supplies, helped in the preparations for Anzio. But the destruction of the German Air Force through the bombing of Axis factories and support of the ground battle when called for were responsibilities which enjoyed higher priority during this period. The Fifteenth began to participate in the Combined Bomber Offensive on German aircraft industries on 20 February 1944, when 126 B-17's were dispatched against Messerschmitt plants at Regensburg-Prüfening. Bad weather prevented them from reaching their objectives. That same day Lt. Gen. Ira C. Eaker, commander of the Mediterranean Allied Air Forces (MAAF), felt obliged to send out half his heavy bombers to provide direct support to the weary ground troops at Anzio.[26]

Strategic air had prepared for the landing at Anzio by strikes at communications centers, particularly railroad yards. On 15 January 1944 Headquarters, Mediterranean Allied Tactical Air Force (MATAF) advised MAAF that the strength of the Strategic Air Force during the period D minus 5 to D-day (16-21 January) could be very usefully applied to the following rail lines, listed in order of priority: a) Florence-Arezzo, b) Empoli-Siena-Arezzo, c) Pisa-Pistoia-Prato-Florence, and d) Rimini-Falconara. Moreover, rail movements and repair work in the vicinity of

Rome, Pisa, and Florence were to be interrupted by night as much as possible.[27] The strategic aircraft were thus charged with establishing an interdiction belt which would halt shipments through the more important rail hubs of west-central Italy about 180 miles north of Anzio. Some 600 effective sorties were flown by heavy bombers in response to these instructions. In the meantime, MATAF bombers were striking similar targets south of Perugia. So few German fighters arose to contest these missions that enemy airdromes received only occasional visits. Nevertheless, on four days between 13 and 21 January, B-17's and B-24's bombed airfields, sometimes, as in the large-scale attack of 13 January on fields at Ciampino and elsewhere in that vicinity, being joined by B-25's and B-26's. On the 21st, strategic aircraft also hit long-range bomber bases in southern France.[28]

On D-day, 22 January, Strategic continued its communications program, though a number of bombers flew against targets in Rome, which was in Tactical's territory. The mediums of MATAF during that day hit communications immediately behind the beachhead. As a result of previous arrangements between Gen. Sir Henry M. Wilson, Allied commander in the Mediterranean theater, and representatives of the various components of MAAF, the Fifteenth was never committed *in toto* to the support of the beachhead, even though General Wilson could have secured such all-out air simply by declaring an emergency. In keeping with General Eaker's strong desire to carry out as soon as possible the obligations of the Fifteenth Air Force to CBO, it was decided informally not to interfere with strategic operations unless a real need should arise, but that then heavy bombers would be assigned to beachhead flights upon application to MAAF.[29]

A true emergency did not develop until mid-February. Nevertheless, long before that time Strategic shifted to more southerly communications targets by way of extending more immediate help to the ground troops. For example, marshalling yards lying in Tactical's area, such as those at Terni, were bombed during the last week of January. Again, when the Germans mounted a few damaging bomber raids, effective attacks were launched against Axis bases in southern France, northern Italy, and Austria. There is no dobut that the interdiction and counter-air work carred out by Strategic significantly delayed Marshal Kesselring's assault on the Allied lodgment.[30] German commanders have testified to the enormous difficulties occasioned by the necessity of rerouting supplies and reinforcements and of unloading and reloading at points in the rail system made impassable by the destruction of bridges or of marshalling yards. The damaging of locomotives was also a severe handicap.[31]

The expected German onslaught opened 16 February and raged for nearly four days. Kesselring's failure, despite his advantage in numbers of ground troops, to carry out Hitler's personal orders to drive the Allies into the sea was in no small measure to be ascribed to the Allies' use of their air weapon. At the very climax of the battle, 17 February, more than 800 aircraft of all types, including 288 heavy bombers, rained 1,000 tons of bombs on enemy positions in the battle area. The 288 heavies not only continued important communications strikes at such places as Campoleone and up the road to Albano Laziale, but they also joined the mediums in bombing positions near the front lines. And for several days thereafter, weather permitting, varying numbers of heavies added to the pressure maintained in close-in communications centers.[32]

On 29 February the Germans surged forward again, and the Fifth Army on 2 March requested additional air protection from MAAF. For its part, the Fifteenth flew 297 effective sorties with 241 B-24's and 100 B-17's. These planes dropped fragmentation bombs along the front on troop concentrations, stores depots, bivouac areas, gun positions, and similar objectives. The Germans for the second time were stopped and forced back on the defensive.[33] It is unquestionably true that the Anzio beachhead failed to accomplish its stated purpose of weakening the Gustav Line so that the Allies could break out quickly and head for Rome. But it is equally certain that air power was a highly important factor in preventing Anzio from turning into an Allied disaster.[34]

During the period 16 to 21 February and the first few days in March, a total of 1,482 heavy bomber sorties were dispatched against close-in and general support targets at Anzio. Because of bad weather only 63 per cent or 933 bombers were able to locate and bomb their objectives. Altogether, 1,858 tons of 20-pound fragmentation and 500-pound general-purpose bombs fell in the 25 separate attacks, a good many of them directed against troop concentrations. Antiaircraft fire was intense in the battle area, accounting for 13 planes lost, 3 missing, and no fewer than 125 damaged. The targets were missed completely in 28 per cent or 7 of the 25 attacks, and the results on the other 18 targets were assessed officially as 1 excellent, 6 good, 10 fair, and 1 poor.[35] The rating "excellent" was given when the photographs of the bomb pattern dropped by a heavy bombardment group showed more than 50 per cent of the visible bomb bursts to be within 1,000 feet of the specified aiming point, "good" when 30 to 50 per cent of the bursts were within that circle, "fair" when the proportion was 20 to 30 per cent, and "poor" when smaller than 20 per cent.[36] The over-all results of the 25 attacks, then, especially in view of the 7 targets that were missed entirely, could not be considered satisfactory.

The evaluation board, in its study of the Anzio bombing, ascribed the below-standard accuracy to a lack of sufficient target information.[37] Yet there is some doubt whether even a higher degree of accuracy on the part of the strategic bombers would have markedly improved the ground situation. The evidence supplied by prisoner interrogation suggests that though the battlefield bombing, including attacks by all classes of aircraft, appreciably damaged the enemy's potential and his morale by battering his tank columns, gun positions, and command posts, immobilizing combat units seeking to move into line, and the like, it yet caused relatively few casualties.[38]

Cassino. While the VI Corps was fighting at Anzio for its existence, the bulk of Gen. Mark Clark's Fifth Army struggled valiantly to break through the Gustav Line and effect a juncture with the beleaguered beachhead. One of the key defenses which foiled this effort was the town of Cassino and its nearby hill, surmounted by the famous Monte Cassino monastery founded in the early sixth century by St. Benedict of Nursia. To support his offensive, General Wilson ordered two massive aerial bombardments: the first on 15 February 1944 of the monastery hill, and the second of the town of Cassino on 15 March. Because neither attack was followed by the hoped-for breakthrough or even by any very substantial gains, the wisdom of this employment of bombers was seriously questioned.

The whole controversy need not be reviewed here, however, since the present concern is mainly with the efficiency with which the heavy bombers carried out the immediate tasks assigned to them in the two actions.[39] The Cassino bombardments were an effort to neutralize an enemy strongpoint by very heavy air attack, the first such operation to be examined in this study, although it bears resemblances to the far more successful Pantelleria bombing. Both the monastery hill and the town were tactical targets, and the town was the clearest possible example of a close-suppprt objective: Allied troops had to be withdrawn 1,000 yards before the planes could unload their bombs.

Prior to the bomber effort at Cassino, the Fifteenth Air Force was not called upon to supplement Tactical Air Force activities on behalf of the Fifth Army facing the Gustav Line. But on 15 February, General Eaker, in response to Wilson's request, relieved 136 B-17's from their other commitments. Together with more than 100 mediums, the heavies bombed the monastery buildings of Monte Cassino, contributing 302 tons out of the total of 576 tons released.[40] The aerial attacks were interspersed with artillery fire, and the combined bombardment almost completely wrecked the ancient abbey buildings. Nevertheless, the Allied ground forces were frustrated in their efforts to take the hill. The additional weight which the strategic bombers lent to the attack was plainly insufficient to quell the defenders.[41]

This failure brought forth considerable criticism from higher headquarters of the use of air power in Italy. Under the belief that a better directed and even more massive assault would succeed, Wilson and his subordinates planned the bombing of Cassino despite General Eaker's reservations about such a project.[42] During the morning of 15 March the whole of Tactical and more than 320 heavy bombers from the Fifteenth dropped approximately 1,000 tons of bombs on the town, covering an area of a fraction of a square mile. The target was smashed, although a number of hitches such as a number of the heavy bomber flights failing to meet schedule, developed. Because dust from previous bomb bursts reduced visibility, 42 of the heavies did not release their bombs at all, and a number of B-24's, likewise confused by dust and smoke, dropped 125.5 tons on friendly areas at Venafro, Villarotunda, and also north of Cassino. Altogether, 262 B-17's and B-24's released 787 tons of 1,000-pound general-purpose bombs with results assessed from poor to fair. No bombers were lost or missing in the action, and only three received battle damage.[43] The post-bombardment ground attack was late in starting, and German troops sheltered in the ruins of the town were able to stem the advance of the New Zealanders who led the attackers. Even after eight days of fighting, the Allies held neither the monastery hill nor the whole of the village of Cassino. It is true that craters and rubble impeded the advance, but perhaps the principal lesson learned from this failure was that such a close-support air effort would probably be wasted unless ground forces could immediately attack the enemy in the bombed area.[44]

The showing of the heavy bombers in this operation was so unsatisfactory from the standpoint of maintaining schedule and bombing accuracy that Eaker ordered an investigation. The results showed that the heavies performed poorly because of the smoke and dust pall and also because of bomb-rack malfunctioning in two of the groups. The bomber crews seem

AHS-88, Chap. III

to have been affected not so much by the fact that they were operating in an unfamiliar tactical role (their bomb runs were made from something near their normal altitude of 15,000 feet) as by other factors which might easily have caused a poor performance against strategic targets. The mediums, on the other hand, especially certain groups of B-26's, made excellent records against Cassino.[45]

An Allied Force Headquarters analysis of the Cassino action stated that now new lessons had emerged from that experience. Rather the established principles of air support merely received confirmation: the follow-up of the infantry attack had to be immediate, aerial bombardment alone was insufficient to clear the enemy from well dug-in positions, heavy bombing produced craters and masses of rubble which impeded infantry movements, and provision should be made for bomb-line markers. It was further noted that the support rendered by tactical aircraft was better than that furnished by strategic bombers. The heavies would have made a better record had the mission been more carefully planned, with particular reference to providing for familiarization flights over the area to be hit and specifying more exactly the angles of approach and the bombing altitudes. Cassino, the report concluded, was not to be considered an indictment of the value of heavy bombers in close support. Rather, it demonstrated that well understood principles of air support must be more fully observed in the planning of such missions.[46]

One might conclude, in retrospect, that since the heavies contributed less than their proportionate share to the already overabundant destruction, the ground assault at Cassino might have gone better without the participation of the B-17's and B-24's. On the other hand, the fact that the follow-up by ground forces was slow renders such a conclusion hazardous.

Operation DIADEM. The all-out offensive of 11 May to 22 June 1944, coded DIADEM, which succeeded in breaking the stalemate in southern Italy and eventually in pushing the Germans behind the Gothic Line in the north, was preceded by an extensive interdiction effort called STRANGLE, a name also used later for a similar operation in Korea. The object of STRANGLE was to impede the flow of enemy supplies to the battle front by means of a vigilantly maintained interdiction of rail lines and highways so that the Germans could not withstand a vigorous ground assault. Not only railroad yards, but also tunnels, defiles, stretches of track, and especially bridges were hit in an unrelenting assault, the full impact of which did not become evident until after the opening of the ground offensive on 11 May. Strategic air power played a small but important role in STRANGLE, inasmuch as it was heavily engaged on a first-priority basis with CBO targets in southern Germany and Austria. But when weather or other obstacles scrubbed such strategic missions, as during the last week in March, the Fifteenth's bombers in company with those of the RAF 205 Group ranged over marshalling yards at Padua, Genoa, Turin, Verona, Milan, and Rimini. An occasional attack on Axis air bases at the head of the Adriatic and in southern France also helped STRANGLE by reducing still further the enemy's air strength. In all, it has been computed that MASAF's aid to the interdiction program amounted to some 5,000 tons of bombs dropped on communications targets, mainly railroad yards. But the principal performers in the "simultaneous interdiction" of enemy supply lines were MATAF's medium, light, and fighter-bombers. Prisoner-of war testimony indicated that fighter-bomber attacks on locomotives and on trains, moving or stationary, were most telling in preventing the movement of supplies to the armies.[47]

Even in Operation DIADEM, the raison d'etre for STRANGLE, few occasions arose on which the heavies of the Fifteenth were diverted from their strategic objectives to work in a tactical capacity. But one of these occasions was especially notable from the standpoint of the number of bombers involved--namely, an attack on 23 May 1944 in which the heavies hit German troop and supply concentrations and also communications at Palestrina, Subiaco, Nemi, and, farther afield, at Avezzano. Figures vary as to the number of sorties flown and the bomb tonnage released, but the AAF Evaluation Board determined that out of the 1,326 airplanes dispatched, 714 located and bombed their objectives, including alternate targets. The large number of non-effective sorties was ascribed to poor weather. A total of 1,889 tons of general-purpose 100- to 2,000-pound bombs fell on the several targets with good over-all results. Three aircraft were lost and 20 damaged. The lack of enemy air resistance and the adequate target information supplied the bombardiers probably accounts for the good record on the part of those bombers which were not blanked out by the weather.[48]

The AAF Evaluation Board did not venture a close appraisal of the above action. Since the carefully selected aiming points were well covered, however, one may assume that the heavies contributed their porportionate share to the breakout of the Allied troops and the routing of the enemy. A directive issued by MAAF on 4 March 1944, just after the second German threat at Anzio had been contained, suggested that much greater tactical employment of heavy bombers had been anticipated in offensive action than proved to be necessary. The directive stated that the progress of the land battle in Italy indicated that the Fifteenth Air Force would, on occasion, have to be employed "against tactical targets directly in support of our land operations," although the "time, method, and frequency of such employment" would depend on the day-to-day tactical situation. The commanding general of MAAF was charged with the responsibility for keeping the commander of MASAF informed as to possible calls for strategic assistance. Should the tactical commander decide that such help was necessary, he was to make his request to MAAF headquarters, which would then issue orders for the attack to MASAF by "redline channels."* [49]

That demands for strategic assistance were held to a minimum is a tribute both to the efficiency of the tactical air groups and to the comprehension on the part of Wilson and his staff of the great importance of the strategic mission of the Fifteenth Air Force.[50] The record of combat reviewed above suggests that these later tactical operations involving heavy bombers, such as that of 23 May, were more carefully and realistically planned as a result of accumulated experience.

Southern France. In the invasion of southern France on 15 August 1944, known first as ANVIL and later as DRAGOON, the relatively smooth and effective performance of the air arm is to be ascribed in part to the absence of air opposition but perhaps even more to the fact that the lessons learned in the earlier Mediterranean landings, particularly Sicily and Salerno, as well as in the great Normandy invasion of 6 June, were heeded by the planners. The Fifteenth's strategic bombers were destined to play a prominent role in each of the several phases of the operation.

In preparation for DRAGOON, Strategic flew a number of missions during July, hitting railroad bridges and yards, submarine pens, harbor installations, and airdromes. These targets were located at Toulon and

---

*   "Redline" messages enjoyed a special treatment and were given high priority by communications offices.

Marseilles on the Mediterranean and as far north as Valence, a good 100 miles behind the invasion beaches. In accordance with Phase 1 of the air plan for DRAGOON, which was devoted to counter-air and interdiction activities, heavy bombers as well as mediums hit points on the rail line between Lyons and the mouth of the Rhône on 2 August, creating a number of blocks. Again, on 6 August, 1,069 bombers attacked railroads, bridges, and yards at transportation centers like Avignon and Arles. In Phase 2 of the preparation, coded NUTMEG and extending from D minus 5 to 1350 hours on D-day, MASAF carried out its commitments by striking 102 gun positions in several different areas: Genoa, Savona, Toulon, Marseilles, and Sète. Out of a total of 1,504 heavy bombers sent on this mission, 1,353 dropped 3,926.5 tons of 500- and 1,000-pound general-purpose bombs. On 51 of the targets, photo-interpreters classified the concentration of bombs as excellent, on 19 as good, on 9 as fair, and on 7 as poor, whereas 13 targets were missed altogether, and for the other 3 no photo coverage was available. In this action, 4 bombers were lost and 30 damaged. The bomb plots, however, tell a somewhat misleading story. The Ordnance Division of the AAF Evaluation Board which inspected the targets shortly after the landings determined that the actual effectiveness of the aerial bombardment of coastal defenses was questionable. Even the near-misses, it was found, often failed to damage the guns, and the same was true of a few hits on the reinforced concrete emplacements. Perhaps the chief benefit of the heavy attack on the guns was that a number of gun crews were panicked into abandoning their posts. The report further specified that although one bomb plot showed a nearly perfect concentration of 97.7 per cent of the hits within a radius of 1,000 feet of the gun position, the gun itself was undamaged because the nearest bomb bursts were about 500 feet away. The board concluded that such pinpoint targets were not well suited to the heavy bombers, which normally released from high altitude.[51]

At 0500 hours on D-day, 15 August, Phase 3, or YOKUM, began with an attack by both heavies and mediums on the assault beaches. Thick weather proved to be a considerable handicap. For example, 30 B-17's and 114 B-24's were unable to get to the beaches on schedule, and an additional 24 B-17's sent out against a gun position were likewise prevented from bombing because of weather. Still, 89 B-17's and 160 B-24's managed to drop 465 tons of 250- and 500-pound bombs, some of them by instruments. No bombers were lost or damaged in combat action although take-off accidents occurred. On its inspection tour of the beaches, the evaluation board learned that even though some of the enemy troops were driven from their positions by the bombing, the over-all effectiveness of the attack was at least as questionable as had been the earlier attempt to pinpoint the guns. One unexpected result was that the beach bombardment, rather than detonating enemy mines, tossed them about so as to create an even greater hazard. On the other hand, the bombing appears to have destroyed some underwater obstacles and to have contributed to the disorganization of enemy defenses.[52] The heavies did not accompany the landing forces themselves when they hit the beaches just east of Toulon at 0800 hours, and the next day MASAF sent its bombers back to CBO targets.

On the whole, the value of Strategic's part in the softening of the invasion beaches must be considered controvertible despite its technically fine performance during the three days preceding the landings. Against the gun positions and similar pinpoint objectives, fighter-bombers were undeniably much more effective. On the other hand, the success of the interdiction carried out during July and earlier in August is beyond dispute. Any plans the Germans may have made to send reinforcements quickly into southern France were rendered impossible of achievement by the blocked communications.

Rumania. For several months beginning in August 1944 MASAF flew missions in aid of the Russian advance through the Balkans. One such mission--the bombing of German installations near Bucharest--had especially clear tactical implications. The strike was flown as the result of a plea from the Rumanian general staff for direct aid in the face of German air attacks which had been provoked by Rumania's withdrawal from the war several days previously.

On 26 August one wave of the Fifteenth's heavies, 114 B-17's dropped 205 tons of 100-pound bombs on German barracks, military stores, and gun positions at Baneasa north of Bucharest. The second wave, consisting of approximately the same number of B-24's, released 258 tons of 500-pound bombs on Otopeni airdrome, which was currently being used by German aircraft engaged in harassing the city of Bucharest. In this action one American airplane was lost and three more were missing. Both attacks appear to have crippled the enemy, especially the assault on the barracks which, according to reports, the Rumanian troops were thereafter enabled to attack successfully.[53] Other Rumanian missions were flown later against marshalling yards and railroad bridges for the purpose of interdicting the routes used by the Germans and thus assisting the Russians.[54]

Bologna. Much more spectacular were two air attacks on Bologna and vicinity in October 1944 and April 1945. The object of both was to blast open Kesselring's line in front of the Fifth Army. As part of the general offensive, which was initiated by the Eighth Army in the east, the Fifth Army pressed northward on 9 September 1944 toward the valley of the Po. But the German defenses held some 12 miles below Bologna. In order to meet Army requests for a great aerial bombardment of enemy installations and troops concentrated here, MATAF called on the resources of MASAF. The heavy bombers accordingly were diverted from their CBO and more northerly communications objectives, and on 12 October 1944, 826 B-17's and B-24's set out to smash targets in the Bologna area, the heaviest single effort yet to be made by the Fifteenth in support of ground troops. The 10 targets consisted of stores depots, barracks, bivouac areas, ammunition dumps, and a munitions factory.[55]

Of the 826 aircraft dispatched, 695 found their targets, on which they poured 1,294 tons of 20-pound fragmentation and 250- and 500-pound general purpose bombs. In the course of the action 3 planes were lost and 49 damaged, but the excellent photographic coverage of the mission by AAF and also by Fifth Army photographers showed that the bombers did their assigned work exceptionally well. The bomb plots on the 10 targets were classified as follows: 2 excellent, 4 good, 2 fair, and 2 poor. But more revealing than such statistics were eyewitness accounts by prisoners to the effect that the bombing created considerable disorganization and havoc, although the prisoners could not as a rule distinguish the attacks made by strategic bombers from those made by tactical aircraft. The Fifth Army analysis specified the great physical damage brought about and concluded that "The air support of the Fifth Army on 12 October

1944 was eminently successful. Assigned targets were attacked in a timely, accurate and most effective manner, thus aiding materially the advance of the Fifth Army in taking valuable terrain."[56] Again, however, this report did not seek to differentiate the bombing of strategic from that of tactical planes.

In spite of this success, the weary ground forces, hindered to some extent by bad weather, were unable to take the city of Bologna and forge ahead to join the Eighth Army, and the Allies endured yet another winter on the "forgotten front." The second full-scale offensive, falling in April, was completely successful, however, and Kesselring's army, trapped at the Po River by the incessant interdiction effort, finally surrendered on 2 May 1945. As their part of WOWSER, the air phase of the spring offensive, the bombers of the Fifteenth flew a number of highly effective missions between 9 and 18 April 1945. Guided by radio and visual aids, 2,052 sorties struck targets along the front lines and in the vicinity of Bologna. The ground forces followed up the bombing quickly, and between 20 and 23 April the heavies finished off the bridges ahead of the retreating enemy. The lessons learned in earlier operations, especially in the use of navigational aids and safety precautions, were not forgotten in the planning of the heavy bomber phase of WOWSER, and were probably responsible for its being the most successful action of its type in the whole of the Italian campaign.[57]

During the nearly four years of warfare in north Africa and Italy, strategic bombers performed tactical functions on a number of important occasions. Throughout this period, for example, the heavies bombed minor communications targets that in terms of AAF doctrine would be regarded as tactical. There was also a tendency, especially during the African phase, for the heavies to be sent against small ships, airdromes within reach of tactical bombers, and similar "unworthy" targets. Direct support to ground troops on or very near the front lines was most successfully carried out at Salerno, Anzio, and Bologna, to judge from official evaluations of those actions. At Cassino the bombs dropped by the strategic aircraft were of questionable value, primarily because of the belated follow-up attack by the ground forces. It must be noted, however, that even when the B-17's and B-24's performed very well according to the photographs of the bomb plots, the ground troops were sometimes unable, because of their depleted state or bad weather, to follow up the bombardment quickly enough to reap the full benefits.

The Italian campaign reveals, on the whole, an improved understanding of the use of air power. The most important lesson of the war in Italy bearing on the tactical use of heavy bombers was that saturation bombing, to be fully effective, should be followed immediately by a strong ground assault. It was also clear long before the final surrender of Kesselring that, next to their purely strategic mission, the role in which the heavies functioned most successfully was in long-range communications strikes such as STRANGLE.[58]

AHS-88

Chapter IV
THE EUROPEAN THEATER

Two differences between operational conditions in the European and Mediterranean theaters were particularly important to the employment of strategic air power. Firstly, industrial Germany, supplying as she did the necessary materiel for three battle fronts, presented an immeasurably richer array of strategic targets than north Africa or even Italy. Secondly, aerial warfare in the Mediterranean developed alongside and remained a concomitant of ground warfare for several years, whereas in the European theater the year of land conflict which brought victory in Europe was preceded by a long period during which the Allied bomber offensive constituted the only contact with the enemy. With the exception of CROSSBOW, the desperate and largely ineffectual attempt to halt the launching of V-weapons against Britain, virtually all strikes made against the Axis in France, Germany, and the Low Countries prior to the invasion of the continent on 6 June 1944 could properly be called strategic. In this assault, all tactical bombers in the United Kingdom participated in a strategic role along with the armada of RAF and Eighth Air Force heavies. But after D-Day, strategic air power in its turn was, on important occasions, committed to tactical operations.

The bomber resources of the Allies in June 1944, the month of the Normandy landings, were enormous. In the United Kingdom, the Eighth Air Force had on operational status approximately 2,100 B-17's and

B-24's, and the RAF Bomber Command 1,100 heavies, while an additional 1,200 strategic bombers of the Fifteenth Air Force were striking the Axis from their bases in Italy.[1] The Eighth and Fifteenth, components of Lt. Gen. Carl Spaatz's United States Strategic Air Forces in Europe (USSTAF), carried out CBO directives as formulated by the Combined Chiefs of Staff until 14 April 1944, on which date operational control passed directly to Supreme Headquarters, Allied Expeditionary Forces (SHAEF). The entire weight of the strategic air weapon was thus placed at General Eisenhower's disposal, should he need it to supplement his tactical air power during and after the invasion. The tactical effort of the Fifteenth Air Force was largely absorbed by the ground campaign in Italy and by the landings in southern France. The Eighth's bases, however, were close enough to the Normandy invasion areas and the later battlefields of northern France to permit giving direct aid to the march on the Reich. For the purpose of coordinating its tactical activities, the Eighth was represented in the headquarters of the Allied Expeditionary Air Forces, the agency which, under ACM Sir Trafford Leigh-Mallory, directed both the U.S. Ninth and the RAF Second Tactical Air Force.[2]

Under such arrangements, which remained in force until 15 September 1944, the Eighth's B-17's and B-24's could readily have been committed *in toto* to direct aid of the ground forces during a good part of the gigantic ground campaign which opened in June 1944. The fact that the Eighth was, with sporadic although important exceptions, allowed to continue its offensive against oil and other industrial and economic objectives during most of this period is an indication of the awareness in SHAEF, especially on the part of General Eisenhower himself, of the overriding importance of strategic bombing.[3] Some notion of that proportion of the total effort of the Eighth Air Force during 1944 which may be classified as tactical is afforded by the following table of bomb tonnages, taken from an Eighth Air Force report:[4]

Total tonnage of bombs expended
    by the 8th Air Force, 1944 . . . . 429,162 tons
        Strategic targets: aircraft factories,
          synthetic oil and chemical plants,
          armament plants, ball-bearing plants 173,000
        Tactical targets: marshalling yards,
          bridges, naval facilities, and
          inland canals 122,255
          fuel dumps 4,005
          V-1 sites 28,771
          experimental sites (Peenemunde etc.) 2,334
          miscellaneous industrial plants 50,092
          targets of opportunity 9,612
          ordnance depots 3,142
          tactical cooperation with ground forces . . . 35,951
Total tonnage expended in tactical operations 256,162

If the broad interpretation of tactical represented in the above table is accepted, it would appear that approximately 60 per cent of the Eighth Air Force's 1944 bomb tonnage fell on tactical objectives. If, however, one classifies "experimental sites" and "miscellaneous industrial plants" as strategic, where they would belong according to AAF doctrine, the proportion of tactical activity falls to 47 per cent. Communications targets of all kinds absorbed 28 per cent, but the cooperation missions flown in 1944 took only 35,591 tons, or less than 10 per cent of the Eighth's total bomb expenditure. In the present chapter, six missions in this last group, close cooperation with ground, receive special study. These missions took place in conjunction with the invasion of Normandy and with the ground battles at Caen, Saint-Lo, Metz and Thionville, Eschweiler, and in the Ardennes. Attention is also paid to the communications strikes of the strategic bombers from June 1944 to May 1945.

Normandy. The air phase of the historic Normandy landings has been described in detail in readily available publications.[5] Here, it is necessary only to single out the tactical tasks allotted to the heavy bombers, esepcially to those of the Eighth Air Force.

The preinvasion air operations fell into three phases. The first of these, extending from D minus 50 to D minus 30, was the counter-air force and reconnaissance phase. The second, D minus 30 to D minus 1, was the preparation for the assault; and the third comprised the softening and interdiction activities immediately before and during the assault itself. Even though strategic air power had been placed under the control of SHAEF on 14 April, the Eighth continued to bomb strategic targets in accordance with directives handed down by ACM Sir Arthur W. Tedder until 1 June.

The priorities of the Eighth Air Force, however, did not remain unaltered during this tense period in world history, nor were all of the objectives allotted to the heavies strategic. Strategic priorities shifted continually from synthetic oil complexes to airframe and engine factories and ball-bearing plants to railroad marshalling yards, bridges, and miscellaneous communications targets. And, on many occasions, CROSSBOW targets, the V-1 launching sites, absorbed the full tonnage of the B-17's and B-24's. Other targets prior to D-Day were enemy airfields and coastal gun positions. Meanwhile, of course, the Fifteenth Air Force was striking communications centers in southern France.[6]

D-Day activities were complex and were rendered even more difficult by the fact that bad weather forced bombardiers to release on instruments rather than visually. The original assault plans envisaged the use of tactical bombers only over the beaches, but when it became plain that the bomb tonnage required was far beyond the capacity of available tactical bombers, the Eighth Air Force and the RAF Bomber Command were called in. RAF heavies on the night of 5 June began the assault phase by area bombing of gun positions along the Cherbourg peninsula and east of the extreme limit of the five landing beaches.[7]

The D-Day activities of the Eighth fall conveniently into four different missions. On the first mission, the softening of the three British beaches, Juno, Sword, and Gold, and of the American beach Omaha, 1,361 heavies were dispatched between 0155 and 0529 hours on 6 June. The difficult assemblies were made according to plan, and in six-squadron-abreast formations behind pathfinder airplanes the armada streamed toward the coast of Normandy. There, as will be recalled, overcast bombing techniques were employed. But, in order to provide an extra margin of safety for the vast fleet of invasion vessels lying off shore, the release was deliberately delayed 10 seconds beyond the H2X-scope indication of the water line, a factor of the utmost importance in assessing the effectiveness of this operation. Between 0555 and 0730 hours, 1,083 B-17's and B-24's dropped nearly 3,000 tons of high explosive and fragmentation bombs, instantaneously fuzed to avoid cratering, from an altitude of 14,000 to 18,000 feet. Of these, 1,015 bombers hit the beaches, 47 attacked chokepoints in the city of Caen just south of one of the British beaches, and 21 were obliged to drop on alternate targets because of navigational troubles. Only one bomber was lost to enemy action and that to anti-aircraft fire. The single instance of short bombing resulted in no damage to friendly forces. The bomb patterns were found to be well concentrated, but, as should have been expected in view of the delayed instrument releases, they lay behind the beaches for distances varying from 300 yards to as much as 3 miles. Beach-line defenses, therefore, were little disturbed by this effort. The principal virtue of this attempt to soften the beaches has been said to lie in the demoralizing effect of the bombardment on the defenders.[8]

The second mission was mounted as soon as possible after the return of the heavies from their preassault bombing. A total of 528 aircraft was sent out to hit chokepoints in a number of towns near the landing beaches. Even though 10/10 cloud conditions still prevailed over Normandy, only one pathfinder was available for this mission. It is not surprising, then, that only three groups, those led by the pathfinder, located their targets in the town of Argentan and bombed. The remaining seven groups returned their bombs to their bases. No aircraft were lost to enemy action, although a collision in the air destroyed two of them.[9]

The third D-Day attack by heavy bombers was directed against two junctions in Caen. Led by a pathfinder airplane, 73 B-24's, of which 56 managed to bomb, flew over Normandy. Again there were no combat losses, but the results, in view of later attacks on the same targets, could not be appraised.[10]

Because of the inadequacy of the second mission described above, a fourth D-Day mission was mounted to strike communications in towns such as Coutances and Lisieux south and east of the beaches. The cloud cover was still heavy, interfering with the assembly of the bombers, yet 553 aircraft, led by 39 pathfinders, attacked over clouds ranging from 5/10 to 10/10. Some bombardiers were able to make visual drops, others bombed on H2X. In all, 437 released on primary targets and the remaining 116 on alternates with results ranging from poor to good. No bombers were lost in this strike.[11]

The heavy bomber attacks just outlined were, of course, supplementary to the all-out efforts of the mediums and the fighter-bombers on D-Day. The Ninth Air Force, for example, assumed responsibility for the preassault bombing of Utah Beach, a task which the mediums had to carry out at a very low altitude because of the overcast. Thereafter, the Ninth Air Force bombers were fully occupied with communications and coastal batteries, and the IX Fighter Command, along with the RAF Second Tactical Air Force, began close ground support. To estimate with any plausible degree of accuracy the Eighth's contributions to the over-all success of the air operations of D-Day is difficult if not impossible. Complaints were received from V Corps that the sharp opposition encountered on Omaha Beach proved the inadequacy of Eighth Air Force bombing, but such complaints could have been anticipated as soon as it was known that visual bombing was not possible. Other reports noted that the demoralizing effects of the bombing of the beaches, if not the resulting physical destruction, was of no small importance to the advance of the ground forces.[12] Very likely, the bombing of roads and bridges along the routes leading to the beaches was of at least equal significance, as had been true at Salerno and Anzio. It is easy to say in retrospect that the 4,778 tons of bombs which the Eighth Air Force delivered on interdiction and close-support objectives on 6 June 1944 could have been better placed, but there can be no question that the enemy was punished and hampered by the effort of the heavy bombers.[13]

Caen. With the fall on 27 June of virtually the last enemy fort in the city of Cherbourg, the U.S. First Army was able to begin a serious effort to move out of the peninsula toward the south. In the meantime, the British and Canadian armies were halted in their push to the east by very strong enemy positions in the outskirts of Caen. The enemy stand at Caen was stubborn, and on three separate occasions attacks by heavy bombers, in addition to the constant activity of tactical bombers, were required before the Allies could resume their drive.

The first major air assault on the Caen defenses was arranged on Montgomery's request. Beginning late on 7 July the RAF Bomber Command performed area bombing of the city, and early the next day IX Bomber Command mediums were flown at troop concentrations and at bridges in the vicinity. This bombardment, supplemented by shelling from naval units, caused such cratering that the ground attack launched late in the day on 8 July was somewhat hampered. Nevertheless, some advances were made into the city.[14] When the Allied found themselves still unable to break through all the Caen defenses and the adjacent hedgerow country, a second heavy bomber attack was laid on in which both the RAF Bomber Command and the Eighth Air Force participated. Early on 18 July approximately 1,000 RAF heavies plastered the area; then 643 B-24's of the Eighth Air Force were dispatched against some of the same targets. Because of the difficulty of proper target identification, six squadrons of B-24's refrained from dropping. The remaining 571 released 1,425 tons of bombs, of which only 26 per cent fell in the assigned area. Again, British naval units directed fire on the city from the Seine Bay. The mediums of the Ninth Air Force which followed up the attacks of the heavies were handicapped by dense smoke and dust over the gun positions constituting their targets. Despite the low score achieved by the American heavies, the British Second Army advancing to the attack immediately after the cessation of the bombing found the enemy in front of them dazed and somewhat demoralized by the concussion of the aerial assault. A very few miles beyond, however, the Allies were again bogged down, both by pouring rain and by a new and more formidable enemy line.[15] It was apparent that the heaviest bomber effort of the Normandy campaign had produced only limited improvement in the ground situation.

In early August, Allied successes elsewhere in Normandy, especially General Patton's advance toward Argentan, led to a renewal of the assault on FM Günther von Kluge's lines in the Caen area. The ground attack was preceded on the night of 7 August by an aerial bombardment delivered by approximately 1,000 RAF heavies. Because bad weather forced many of the RAF aircraft to land at bases other than their own after the initial bombing, the Eighth Air Force was asked to participate in the strategic-bomber support of the ground action planned for 8 August. On this date, 678 B-17's were dispatched at an altitude of 12,000 to 14,000 feet against close-support objectives along a bomb line running 1,700 yards beyond the nearest friendly troops. The B-17's flying in 3 waves comprised 55 tactical groups of 12 to 13 aircraft each. The bomb line was indicated by flares dropped by pathfinder airplanes and also by artillery smoke, and the RAF marked friendly lines by yellow smoke. From the air, however, none of these devices were visible. It is not surprising, then, that no more than 16 of the tactical groups bombed in or adjacent to the target areas, although 2 other groups hit targets of opportunity in enemy territory. The remaining aircraft fared badly. Nine groups, unable to locate their objectives, returned with their bombs still in the racks, four groups bombed short but in enemy-held territory, and two groups bombed inside friendly lines. This tragic error resulted in 25 deaths and 131 wounded among Polish troops serving with the Canadians.[16] Intense antiaircraft fire brought down 10 B-17's and caused major damage to 107 others and minor damage to 187, making the mission an expensive one for the results achieved. Five minutes after the bombing, the ground attack got under way and made some gains, even though enemy resistance was still strong.[17]

In the missions of 18 July and 8 August at Caen, the Eighth Air Force expended a total of 3,326 tons of bombs against close-support targets. In neither attack did the heavies achieve a satisfactory record of accuracy. The low experience level of the bomber crews, resulting from the 30-mission combat tour then in effect in the ETO, and the intense antiaircraft fire, esepcially on the second mission, could not but have had adverse consequences. The fact that the ground forces made at least limited gains after the bombardment of 8 August must, in part, however, be attributed to the work of the tactical aircraft on the same day.[18]

Saint-Lô. By early July the impetus of the Normandy invasion had carried the Allies southward until they confronted a strong line along the Lessay-Périers-Saint-Lô highway. In an effort to penetrate this line and thus to break out of the Cherbourg peninsula, the Allies planned a massive assault, COBRA, the air preparation for which was to be especially heavy. In particular, both tactical and strategic bombers were to participate in saturating a large enemy-held area just south of the highway marking the battle line. The Army was ready to launch its ground assault on whatever day between 21 and 25 July the weather proved most favorable for air. On the first three of these five days, thick weather caused postponements, but on 24 July, Leigh-Mallory, encouraged by forecasts, ordered the aerial bombardment to being.[19]

The fighter-bombers were sent out to execute the first phase of the assault, but continuing bad visibility caused the recall of half their number and prevented the remainder from observing the results of their own bombs. The next wave, consisting of Eighth Air Force heavies, performed even less well. Although 1,586 bombers took off for the mission, scarcely more than 30 per cent, some 484 airplanes, could find their primary targets and bomb. A few of the heavies received Leigh-Mallory's belated recall of the mission before reaching the target area, but nearly all the failures were directly due to the cloud cover. The medium bomber strike which was to follow immediately was canceled before take-off.[20]

Since the ground attack was also scrubbed, no real assessment of the results of the aerial bombardment was possible. The scanty evidence indicated, however, that of 944.5 tons of bombs expended, very few bursts were within the target area, which extended for 5 miles along the highway. According to one estimate, only 15 per cent of the bombs dropped by aircraft of the 1st Bombardment Division, Eighth Air Force, fell within the designated territory. Moreover, there were instances of the bombing of friendly troops. One formation of 16 heavies dropped when the lead airplane, because of mechanical difficulties, make a premature release. The bombs, falling some distance north of the highway, caused 16 deaths and many more wounded among personnel of the 30th Infantry Division. Three bombers were lost in the action.[21]

In the repetition of the COBRA air attack the very next day, extensive precautions were taken against short bombing. Colored artillery smoke was used as before, and, in addition, ground troops withdrew 1,500 yards north of the bomb line and marked their position with panels spread out on the ground. The fighter-bombers and mediums attacked first on this occasion, and then 1,579 B-17's and B-24's flew over the target on a complicated time schedule to deliver 3,400 tons of bombs. Although visibility was better than on the previous day, clouds necessitated bombing from altitudes considerably lower than planned--namely, from approximately 11,200 feet to 13,700 feet. This change involved hurried readjustments of bombsights and probably reduced accuracy somewhat. Despite the precautions taken, short bombing occurred on the part of 35 aircraft with the most dire results. One tactical group of 12 B-24's dropped 470 x 150-pound high-explosive bombs behind friendly lines when the lead bombardier made his visual release without synchronizing his bombsight. Another group of B-24's dropped 352 x 260-pound fragmentation bombs at a point on which the other group had bombed in error. Another blunder occurred when a command pilot, under the impression that bombing was to be done by wings rather than groups, prematurely ordered his bombardier to release. These bombs fell harmlessly in the strip that had been evacuated by friendly forces, but the following group, bombing on this airplane as leader, caused casualties within the American lines. It should be noted, however, that some IX Bomber Command mediums were also guilty of short bombing. No fewer than 101 troops of the same infantry division that had suffered the day before were killed by the short releases, including Lt. Gen. Lesley J. McNair, and 463 were wounded.[22]

Despite the accidental bombing of American lines, the First Army made a breakthrough immediately after the air attack, and in consequence the aerial bombardment has been classed as highly successful. Statistics show that 30 to 35 per cent of the bombs dropped by the heavies fell beyond the target area and 5 to 10 per cent fell short, of which about

3 per cent dropped among American troops. The damage done to the enemy by the remaining 50 per cent of the total bombs, however, was very great, to judge from prisoner-of-war testimony. The greatest gain was the severe strain on enemy morale effected by the virtually unopposed carpet attack. In addition, the cratering of roads and the destruction of other communications had an undeniably powerful influence on the efficiency of the defenses. Finally, some 3 per cent of all enemy personnel were apparently killed outright by the bomb bursts.[23]

The shock of the casualties caused by short bombing prompted earnest research in the interests of perfecting bomber techniques in support operations. In particular, better bomb-line marking and improved air discipline were obviously essential.[24]

Metz-Thionville. The heavy bomber attack of 9 November 1944 on fortresses at Metz and Thionville was the weightiest tactical mission flown by the Eighth Air Force since the conquest of Normandy. Operation MADISON, the offensive mounted by General Patton's Third Army in an effort to break into the Saar district just south of Luxembourg, was impeded by fire from forts at Metz and elsewhere along the Moselle River. Consequently, the XX Corps early in November requested that the Eighth Air Force assist in reducing such strongpoints. Low cloud cover prevented the heavies from hitting the Metz-Thionville installations on their first try on 5 November, and they went on to bomb alternate targets in enemy territory. The ground attack against the Metz salient opened on 8 November with the support of fighter-bombers, and on the 9th the heavies attacked a series of seven forts in the Metz area as well as marshalling yards and other points in three additional cities: Thionville, Saarbrücken, and Saarlautern.[25]

For the protection of American troops, who were at no point closer than four miles to the objectives, an elaborate marking system was devised. Gee-H electronic equipment was used to channel the approaches, which were made as nearly perpendicular to the front lines as possible in order to hold the period over enemy territory to a minimum. In both the Metz and the Thionville areas, a double bomb line was indicated by antiaircraft artillery which fired black bursts to an elevation of 17,000 feet and also by SCS-51 transmitters which actuated indicators in the lead aircraft at the moment they passed directly overhead. Upon passing over and recognizing the bomb line either by the shell bursts or by the radio indicator, the lead airplanes were to fire flares which were then to be acknowledged by the rest of the formation. H2X, or radar-scanning equipment, was to be employed if visual bombing proved impossible.[26]

Because the cloud cover was nearly complete over all objectives, the execution of the mission is of particular interest. Out of nearly 1,300 heavies sent out, 1,233 flying in 3 forces dropped a total of 2,609 tons of bombs from an elevation of 22,000 to 23,000 feet. The SCS-51 marking of the bomb line was found to be superior to the marking by artillery shells, and much of the bombing itself was perforce by H2X. Of the 435 B-17's dispatched by the 1st Bombardment Division against the Metz area, 349 dropped on their primary objectives and 70 on various targets of opportunity. Some releases were visual, others by H2X. Three hundred and forty aircraft of the 401 B-24's of the 2d Bombardment Division, which also flew to Metz, dropped on the assigned targets either visually or by Gee-H calculations. The 459 B-17's of the 3d Bombardment Division were less fortunate, however, since only 37 released on their Thionville objectives, while 308 flew on to Sarrbrucken where they bombed the marshalling yards by H2X. The single instance of short bombing, ascribed to a faulty bomb rack, occurred some 20 miles behind friendly lines but caused no casualties. Four bombers were lost, and 1 sustained major damage and 96 minor damage.[27]

The accuracy record of the mission was very low, chiefly owing to the necessity for bombing by radar, only 1 to 2 per cent of the bombs fell on the Metz objectives. In the Thionville attack, neither of the two primary targets was touched. Nevertheless, reports from the Third Army and prisoner interrogations agree in stating that the over-all effects of the operation were excellent. Diminished fire from the forts that were attacked was ascribed to the demoralization of enemy troops, and attacking infantry, following up the bombardment closely, found the forces in front of them still slightly dazed. Again, the smashing of communications played an important role in reducing German effectiveness. The 5th Infantry Division reported that the big bombers were "eminently successful" in enabling the Third Army to bypass the Metz-Thionville forts. Such results, however, were achieved by the intensity rather than the accuracy of the attack.[28]

Eschweiler. Early in November 1944 the Allies were trying vigorously to break into Germany across the Belgian border near Aachen. Facing the VII Corps of the U.S. First Army were powerful defenses at Aachen,

Eschweiler, and Geilenkirchen, and beyond was the Roer River line. In accordance with instructions issued by the First Army on 26 October 1944, the VII Corps was to advance toward Coblenz on or about 1 November. The strongly fortified positions in front of the First Army indicated the need for a large air attack, and later evidence of an enemy build-up in this area brought about an upward revision of both the ground and air forces required for the advance.[29]

Specific air plans in support of this major Allied offensive were formulated in a series of meetings at IX Tactical Air Command headquarters between 30 October and 7 November by representatives of the 12th Army Group, First and Ninth Armies, Eighth and Ninth Air Forces, and IX and XXIX Tactical Air Commands. It was agreed that heavily fortified positions in the vicinity of Eschweiler and Langerwehe should be hit by Eighth Air Force heavies and those positions around Jülich and Aldenhoven by Ninth Air Force mediums. The RAF Bomber Command would be asked to add its weight to the bombing of built-up areas at Düren and Jülich. Provision was made for a Ninth Air Force attack on Eschweiler targets should the heavies be grounded because of bad weather.

D-day was to fall between 10 and 16 November, and, so that the ground attack could be made during daylight, H-hour was to be not later than 1400 hours. The heavy bombers were to complete their work by H-hour and the mediums were to strike immediately thereafter, but the RAF Bomber Command was given a more flexible schedule because its objectives were farther removed from friendly lines.

The mission of the Eighth Air Force at Eschweiler was to attack "heavy enemy defenses immediately in front of our forces to enable our friendly troops to advance with greater facility and fewer casualties."[30] The objectives assigned to the heavies consisted mainly of very strong concrete emplacements and defended towns. Because the areas in which the towns and fortifications lay were far too large to permit carpet bombing, the most strongly fortified sections were singled out by the Eighth Air Force as aiming points. There were no secondary or last resort targets.[31]

Communications were carefully organized for the big effort. The Army established an air support communications center manned by both air and ground personnel. Since this center maintained radio contact with liaison officers at all division and corps headquarters, the Army command could keep well informed about the air situation in every sector and make requests for air strikes to the appropriate air commanders. The air force, for its part, supplied a mobile forward fighter-control unit to the artillery-control section of each division, and a main fighter-control unit, commanded by a senior pilot with theater experience, to each corps artillery center. The main fighter-control units were especially well provided with radio and radar equipment. Aircraft assigned to close support reported first to the main fighter controller, who either gave them target information directly or turned them over to a forward fighter-control unit for specific targets. The radar operator at the main fighter-control station could veto a strike if it seemed to him too close to friendly lines.[32] This elaborate system was, of course, primarily designed for the control of tactical aircraft, but it was also available for control of the tactical missions flown by the Eighth Air Force heavies, witness the incident* where an accidental release of bombs over friendly territory was so promptly reported by Army sources that all the other bombers could be ordered by radio to close their bomb-bay doors on their return flights to avoid any further delayed releases. The radio communications plan and also the H2X marking system were tested by a practice mission flown over the North Sea on 10 November.[33]

The Eighth Air Force was responsible for providing all radio and radar aids for the protection of the troops from short bombing, and the ground forces were to supply visual aids, such as ground panels and balloons.[34] With an eye to the short bombing tragedy at Saint-Lo, a most comprehensive marking system was used, even though the bomb line was approximately two miles beyond the nearest friendly troops. The bomber crews were briefed on certain H2X checkpoints; buncher beacons† and white ground panels marked an orientation point; and the safety line, two miles inside the most advanced position of friendly troops, was indicated by buncher beacons, by captive balloons, and by antiaircraft bursts 500 yards apart at an elevation 2,000 feet below the briefed altitude of the bombers. Moreover, an SCS-51 localizer transmitter was so adjusted and sited that, upon passing the marker line, each pilot would be informed

---

*See below, p. 93.

†Surface-based, electronic beacons used for positioning a number of aircraft over a given point.

of his position by the response of the dial indicator in front of him. Finally, red and orange panels were laid out 500 yards to the rear of friendly forward lines and for 5 miles on either side of the main axis of attack. Contact with very high frequency (VHF) ground control was to be maintained during the approach to the marker line. Upon recognizing, either by shell bursts 2,00 feet below him or by the SCS-51 signal, that he had crossed the marker line, the leader of each tactical group was to fire flares, which the other planes in the formation had to acknowledge. Acknowledgment had to be completed before the tactical unit was free to release on the target. In the event of nonvisual conditions, the bombers were to release on H2X but for added safety were to continue their bomb runs 30 seconds beyond the indicated release point.[35]

Shortly after noon on 16 November, heavies from all three Eighth Air Force bombardment divisions attacked their targets around Eschweiler and Langerwehe, while RAF bombers struck other towns on the Roer River line. Force No. 1 sent out by the Eighth consisted of 13 tactical groups of 12 to 13 B-17's each belonging to the 3d Bombardment Division, Force No. 2 comprised 14 groups of the 1st Bombardment Division, and Force No. 3, 14 groups of the 2d Bombardment Division. Thick weather over the bases in England prevented one group of the 1st Bombardment Division from taking off and delayed two others. Out of 1,234 heavy bombers readied for the mission, 1,191 dropped their bombs. Each lead squadron had one or more airplanes with Gee-H, Micro-H, and H2X equipment. Because bombs had to be dropped through an 8/10 cloud cover, the accuracy record was low. Of the 3 areas, varying from 225 to 410 acres, assigned to the 1st Bombardment Division, the first received 6 per cent of the bombs directed against it, the second none at all, and the third 16 per cent. On its three targets, the 2d Bombardment Division scored 3 to 11 per cent; and the 3d Bombardment Division 16 per cent. The sole instance of short bombing resulted when one plane's bombs hung up only to work loose over friendly territory. No casualties resulted, but VHF control at once advised all returning bombers to close their bomb-bay doors after completing their runs, a precaution which was to be included in all future instructions for close-in operations. No enemy fighters rose to meet the bombers, and although 62 aircraft sustained damage, none was lost.[36]

The 3,873 tons of fragmentation clusters dropped by the Eighth Air Force on enemy concentrations at Eschweiler and Langerwehe were apparently effective in reducing the fire from field guns, even though casualties inflicted on troops seem not to have been numerous. Moreover, the weight of the attack did not fall on the enemy front lines; hence, the U.S. First Army did not find the defenses before them much softened. The gains made on the ground during the days following the bombardment were small. On the other hand, the destruction wrought at Eschweiler and the fortified places attacked both by the Eighth Air Force and the RAF bombers was enormous, and undoubtedly played a part in weakening the enemy's morale and staying power.[37]

One measure of the effectiveness of the mission, despite the failure of the ground forces to make the hoped for advances, was to be found in the prisoner-of-war testimony. On the basis of such interviews, a First Army special report stated that the bombing caused many enemy units to scatter and prevented AA gunners from giving away their positions by firing. Enemy casualties were highest in two infantry regiments, one of which was in the process of relieving the other in the line when the first bombs fell.[38] It was in recognition of this sort of contribution that Maj. Gen. Terry Allen, commander of the 104th Infantry Division, sent a message of thanks to the Eighth Air Force.[39]

Ardennes. The great attack which the Germans launched on 16 December 1944 in the hilly Ardennes country nearly succeeded in its object of forcing the Allies back to the Meuse River line. Catching the Allied armies by surprise during a prolonged period of nonflying weather, the Germans at least postponed the penetration of the Reich in this sector. Allied infantry and armored reinforcements were thereupon rushed to the battlefield, and General Patton opened a counterattack on the steadily growing enemy salient from the south.[40]

Likewise, transfers of tactical air organizations brought more power to the RAF Second Tactical Air Force, which provided support to the 21 Army Group. And further to increase the air potential in the battle area, the whole of the Eighth Air Force 2d Bombardment Division was placed under the operational control of the Ninth Air Force for the duration of the emergency. Heretofore, the Eighth Air Force had been absorbed in its strategic activities, except for occasional diversions, such as the November missions in the Metz-Thionville and the Eschweiler areas. The peak of the campaign against enemy oil was reached in November although heavy bomb tonnages had at the same time been expended against ordnance depots and tank and motor vehicle factories. By their initial success in the Ardennes, therefore, the Germans forced the Allies to reduce the weight of the bomber assault on oil installations which, as was learned after the war, had become a very sensitive element in the capacity of the

Germans to continue the struggle.[41]

Not until 23 December did weather permit any all-out participation of air power in the Allied defense. Nevertheless, on 18 December, Eighth Air Force heavies began their work of establishing an interdiction line at most points more than 75 miles behind the ground battle. On that day, nearly 1,000 heavies bombed marshalling yards, bridges, and other communications along the Rhine in the vicinity of Cologne, Coblenz, and Mainz. On the next day, a force of approximately one-third that size hit other communications. Clearing weather permitted full-scale operations again on the 24th, when some 1,400 heavies, of which 31 were lost, released 3,506 tons of bombs on a number of enemy airfields. At the same time, an additional 634 bombers returned to communications centers along or near the Rhine. Although the weather grew worse toward the end of the month, the Eighth Air Force continued to send very large forces on interdiction strikes until well into January, when the original battle line had been regained. At no time during the German offensive in the Ardennes were heavy bombers employed in a close-in role. But their blows at transportation and airfields supplemented mightily the more direct support rendered the ground troops by the tactical bombers and fighters. To judge from the statements of enemy generals, the failure of the Germans in the Battle of the Bulge was in considerable part attributable to the Allied use of air power, particularly strategic bombers.[42]

Unlike the other actions described in this chapter, the forty-day Battle of the Bulge did not require the employment of strategic bombers in a direct support role. Nevertheless, the emergency created by the German offensive was sufficiently great to bring about the diversion of approximately one-third the strength of the Eighth Air Force from its strategic work to the task of battlefield interdiction. That the massive blows delivered against communications hampered the enemy seriously there can be no doubt, though to separate the achievements of the strategic from those of the tactical air forces in this category appears impossible.[43]

. . . .

The five instances of the use of heavy bombers in close support described in this chapter--Normandy, Caen, Saint-Lô, Metz-Thionville, and Eschweiler--reveal increasing progress in providing for the safety of friendly ground troops. It is not so clear whether they also indicate any improvement in bombing accuracy on the part of the heavies. The fact that weather conditions necessitated instrument bombing on a large part of these missions may, however, account for the low accuracy record throughout. But, despite the fact that few of the targets were well covered, the strategic bombers performed undeniably important service when used for area bombing of open positions, as at Saint-Lô. And the interdiction of the heavies, especially in the Ardennes, proved to have far-reaching benefits, just as it had in the Italian campaign.[44]

The best available general summary of the effectiveness of the heavies in a tactical role in the ETO is a report prepared by theater commanders. Strategic bombers, this report stated, were employed in four different kinds of tactical operations: 1) bombing in front of the ground attack with the object of destroying or paralyzing the enemy forward defenses to a depth of about 2,000 yards, as at Saint-Lô; 2) bombing of specified areas behind forward hostile defensive systems and isolating forward enemy troops from rear echelons, as at Caen; 3) bombing of defended areas on the flanks of the advance, leaving avenues for our own troops, as at Salerno; and 4) destroying enemy headquarters, concentration areas, or dumps within a few miles of the forward enemy lines, as at Bologna. The uplift to friendly troops brought about by the participation of the heavies was very great, the report continued, and in several actions the work of the strategic bombers was the decisive factor in the success that was achieved. The report concluded on the note that, despite the fact that the use of heavy bombers in a tactical role was new and experimental, it had proved of material value on numerous occasions.[45]

AHS-88

Chapter V

THE PACIFIC AND ASIATIC THEATERS

The Pacific and Asiatic theaters of World War II embraced nearly all the vast expanse of the Pacific Ocean as well as India, Burma, and parts of China. The waging of a war over so large a portion of the earth's surface brought unprecedented problems, not least in the use of air power. For example, except for limited activities in Burma, China, and Borneo, strategic objectives were accessible only during the last months of the war, when the B-29's were finally able to reach the cities and industries in the home islands of Japan.[1] Before that time, with infrequent exceptions, the principal role of the heavy bombers was the execution of long-range strikes at Japanese air and sea power. Plainly, the employment of strategic bombers in the Pacific and Asia differed radically from that already described in the Mediterranean and European theaters of operation. Even the close-support missions flown by the heavies in the Pacific were few, for reasons that are touched on later.[2] The general pattern of heavy and very heavy bomber activity is here described as it developed in each of the several combat areas of the war against Japan. Attention is also given to several actions in the island campaigns which involved the use of heavy bombers in close support.

The necessity of dividing the great reaches of the Pacific into theaters or areas of operations was apparent early in the war. In April 1942 the areas and commands were outlined as follows:

1) Southwest Pacific Area (SWPA). Included the Philippines, Australia, New Guinea, the Bismarck Islands, the western part of the Solomons, and the surrounding waters to the coast of China. All forces in this area were under Gen. Douglas MacArthur, Commander in Chief, SWPA.

2) Southeast Pacific Area (SEPA). Included the coastal waters west of Central and South America down to the South Pole. This area was patrolled by a small fleet under the command of Rear Adm. John F. Shafroth.

3) Pacific Ocean Areas (POA). Included everything between and north of SWPA and SEPA. Adm. Chester W. Nimitz was commander in chief of all forces operating in POA, which was in turn divided into:

   A. North Pacific Area Command (NOPAC). Included the Aleutians and Alaska and all waters north of latitude 42 degrees north. The United States forces, naval and army, in this area were commanded by Rear Adm. Robert A. Theobald and later by Vice Adm. Thomas C. Kinkaid.

   B. Central Pacific Area Command (CENPAC). Included the Hawaiian, Gilbert, Marshall, Caroline, and Mariana islands and all waters south of NOPAC to the equator. Admiral Nimitz retained direct personal command of this important area.

   C. South Pacific Area Command (SOPAC). Included the Ellice, Phoenix, Marquesas, Tuamotu, Samoa, Fiji, and New Hebrides islands, the eastern part of the Solomons (including Guadalcanal), and the islands of New Caledonia and New Zealand, and waters south of the equator to the Pole.

Vice Adm. Robert L. Ghormley commanded the SOPAC Force and Area, but was succeeded on 20 October 1942 by Vice Adm. William F. Halsey.

4. China-Burma-India theater (CBI). Here, United States commitments were largely in the form of air power and logistical aid.[3]

United States air forces were allotted to the various theaters of the war with all possible speed after Pearl Harbor, and a pattern of combat employment began to emerge. A notion of the general uses to which heavy bombers were put may be furnished by a brief résumé of the course of the air war as it was waged by each of the air forces in the Pacific and Asia.

NOPAC: Eleventh Air Force

Although the actual fighting in the North Pacific Area, which was consistently regarded as a defensive rather than an offensive theater, lasted only a short time and involved relatively light forces, air power, including strategic bombers, was used there in much the same fashion as in other more important theaters in the Pacific. The presence of the Japanese in the Aleutians was first made known when their carrier planes bombed Dutch Harbor on 3 June 1942. The Eleventh Air Force, Brig. Gen. William O. Butler commanding, struck back promptly. Under the operational control of Rear Adm. Robert A. Theobald, planes of the Eleventh's single heavy bombardment squadron took off from Cold Bay, staged through Umnak, and bombed enemy shipping and shore installations on Kiska. The first strike was delivered on 10 June, and subsequent missions were flown whenever the notoriously perverse and dangerous weather of the Aleutians area allowed. On only six occasions between

11 and 30 June could the B-17's and B-24's negotiate the 1,200-mile round trip. Moreover, the results of the bombing could seldom be observed because of the cloud cover. The area commander therefore ordered the discontinuance of such missions for the time being, although there was to be no letup in the long reconnaissance missions flown by the heavies over the Bering Sea. The establishment of American bases at Adak at the end of August and at Amchitka in February 1943 permitted the resumption of the bombing, and because of the proximity of the new bases to Kiska, medium and fighter-bombers also participated.

On 11 May 1943 came the amphibious landings on Attu and with it a bloody battle, in the course of which on three successive days direct support was supplied by B-24's. On 24 May, 5 B-24's of the 36th Squadron, following instructions from another bomber which served both as a liaison and weather plane, dropped their 100-pound bombs on enemy positions from as low as 3,000 feet and then strafed mountain-side trench systems at close range from an altitude of only 1,900 feet. The mission was repeated the next day by another five aircraft, the Chichagof harbor area receiving most of the bombs. Seven other bombers patrolled the east side of the ridge at Chichagof harbor but observed no enemy movements and found the ceiling too low for effective bombing. And on 26 May the 36th Squadron sent out nine B-24's, including the weather plane, on another foray which resulted in hits on gun positions and good concentrations in the target areas. No buildings were left intact in the tiny settlement of Attu. In spite of the extremely low altitudes at which these ground-support attacks were carried out, only one B-24 suffered battle damage.[4]

Compared with the magnitude of operations in the ETO, this series of missions is negligible. Yet these strikes are significant for other reasons: the method, essentially the same as that used in all Pacific campaigns, but not very well suited to the Aleutians operations, that was used to direct the bombers to close-support targets; and the belated means taken to avoid bombing within friendly lines. In all close-support operations, control techniques and safety devices are of primary importance, as the foregoing survey of combat experience in the ETO has amply demonstrated. In relatively simple small-scale actions, such as the Attu support bombing, control methods and safety precautions became even more crucial.

The Aleutians campaign was carried out under a Navy commander—Vice Adm. Thomas Kinkaid. The over-all plan directed that the Eleventh Air Force provide general air support during the Attu landings on 11 May and act later as a reserve striking force.[5] Control of air activities over Attu was effected by a liaison airplane. The Navy commander directed Eleventh Air Force planes to specific targets through the AAF commander of the liaison bomber. For a period of six days at the time of the landings, Brig. Gen. William E. Lynd, AAF officer on Admiral Nimitz's staff, flew the command plane.[6]

General Lynd offered a number of trenchant observations about the Navy's use of air power in preparation for the Aleutian landings and for a few days thereafter. In his opinion, a basic error had been committed in directing air attacks against some 29 targets which the Navy had designated some time before on the basis of aerial reconnaissance. Much of the initial air-support action was wasted, he felt, because some of these targets had been evacuated. Moreover, half the orders from the Navy could not be executed because of local weather conditions, such as cloud cover.[7] In the later direct-support missions of 24 to 26 May, however, intelligence summaries revealed that the B-24 attacks drew blood. Hits were secured on AA batteries, targets of opportunity were well covered, and the strafing by B-24 gunners had a visible effect on the Japanese defenders.[8] The captured war diary of a Japanese medical officer, who along with most of his comrades committed suicide on 29 May, provided most vivid testimony to the punishment meted out by the aerial attacks. As a rule, however, the diarist did not distinguish between the work of the B-24's and that of the P-38's and the medium bombers.[9]

The targets assigned to the B-24's on 24 to 26 May were not infrequently close to friendly troops. On the first of these three days, several bombers flying up the Sarana valley dropped their loads among U.S. troops of the 2d Battalion, 32d Infantry, but by great good fortune no casualties resulted. The spectacle of American bombs falling among their comrades was, however, scarcely helpful to the morale of the infantrymen.[10] On their support missions the next day, B-24 crews could see spread out on the ground beneath them panels spelling out "This is our forward line."[11] This apparently was the only direct measure taken to avoid further instances of short bombing.

It had been hoped that air power would aid materially in breaking the stalemate that developed in the ground battle for Attu shortly after the landings. All evidence indicates that the Eleventh Air Force carried out its commitments successfully and that the close-support work of 24 to

26 May was of some avail. Though no close estimate of the effectiveness with which the B-24's supplemented the work of the mediums and fighter-bombers during this period can be made, the record of the heavy bomber missions suggests that assigned targets were well hit and that the B-24's did at least their share of the close-support tasks in a creditable manner.

The Kiska landings of August 1943 were preceded by softening attacks by all classes of bombers. The fact that the Japanese had already evacuated this island, their last foothold in the Aleutians, deprived the Eleventh of its primary mission. Thereafter, throughout the course of the war against Japan, the now greatly reduced air force sent its bombers against targets on Paramushiru and Shimushu in the Kurils, a program which succeeded in pinning down a sizeable force of enemy aircraft in the Hokkaido-Kurils area.[12]

Clearly, the heavy bombers of the Eleventh Air Force functioned altogether in a tactical capactiy in their long-range strikes against enemy shipping, air bases, and troop concentrations, their reconnaissance missions, and their very minor attack-plane work on Attu. In the complete absence of any strategic targets in NOPAC, they could scarcely have been otherwise employed. Even in the Kurils strikes, the targets were mainly shipping and airdromes.

CENPAC: Seventh Air Force

Air operations in the Aleutians were on a miniature scale compared with those in other parts of the Pacific. The Army air weapon in the Central Pacific Area was the Seventh Air Force, which, under the command of Maj. Gen. Willis H. Hale, was based in Hawaii. After the disaster of

Pearl Harbor, the Seventh was built into a combat force although it never became very large. Except for a small role in the great sea battle of Midway, 4 to 6 June 1942, it made few contacts with the enemy during the first 18 months of the war. The Seventh's principal function during this period was to provide training and engineering services to new units en route to exposed bases farther to the west. In the spring of 1943, however, advanced units of the Seventh were sent to the Ellice Islands to assist in attacks on the Marshalls and on Tarawa; later, it flew both its heavy and medium bombers against many enemy strongholds, including Truk, Guam, and Saipan. On the two last-named islands, as well as on Kwajalein, it established heavy bomber bases. One of its B-24 groups, based in the Palaus, bombed enemy bases in northern Luzon by way of protecting the landings in the Philippines. As the Allies closed in on the home islands, the Seventh was assigned to the Far East Air Forces (FEAF) and moved to Okinawa, from which vantage point it attacked Shanghai air installations in July 1945 and concurrently hit shipping, docks, and a Mitsubishi aircraft factory.[13]

Perhaps the greatest work performed by the B-17's and B-24's of the Seventh was long-range preinvasion bombing of enemy-held islands. For example, on 13 November 1943, 18 B-24's took off from Funafuti Island in the Ellice group to drop 15 tons of fragmentation and general-purpose bombs on the airfield and fortifications on Tarawa in the Gilberts, a round-trip flight of more than 2,000 nautical miles. Only one airplane was lost on the mission. Twelve similar flights were made during the week that followed, and reconnaissance of the Gilbert group was combined with the bomber strikes.[14]

Other blows had been directed sporadically against the Gilberts since April 1943, but the attacks on Betio in the Tarawa atoll in November were the prelude to the Marine landings there on 20 November. In all, 50 sorties hit Betio with bombing results that were assessed as 78 per cent effective; i. e., 78 per cent of the bomb load fell on or near the assigned targets.[15] As has been suggested elsewhere, however, appraisals based on bomb plots provide no certain measure of the actual damage done to installations such as gun emplacements. It is clear that the preinvasion strikes did not knock out the airstrips. Because such airfields as the Japanese had could be readily repaired, complete neutralization could have been maintained only by an impossibly large force of bombers. But despite the fact that the enemy airstrips were usable, the carrier-borne bombers of the Navy task force accompanying the landing troops on 20 November were able to cope with all Japanese air activity.[16]

The disturbing feature about the Tarawa preinvasion attacks was that the Marines found that the softening of the ground defenses had been far from adequate despite the high percentage of hits scored by the heavies and the severe naval shelling which followed. The virtual failure of the softening effort at Tarawa has been more than once studied by experts. The U.S. Strategic Bombing Survey reported that the preliminary air attack was "not sufficiently heavy or concentrated."[17] The AAF Evaluation Board characterized the work of the B-24's as "meager by persistent."[18] In a more critical vein, Lt. Gen. Robert C. Richardson, commander of Army forces in CENPAC, observed that the scattered bombing of targets on several different islands represented "an undesirable dissipation of air power." He believed that better results would have been obtained had AAF doctrine been followed—that is, had all available air power been directed against one target until it was destroyed and then shifted to a second objective.[19]

Finally, a Marine historian wrote that to be effective, "the preparatory bombing and shelling to be delivered on enemy-held islands similar to Betio would have to be increased in duration and weight, all of this with an eye toward the total destruction of accurately located weapons and fortifications." But the same report pointed out that "those who believed, before Tarawa, that planes and ships could destroy completely the enemy fortifications on a small coral island were quick to perceive their error."[20] This officer, although advocating a far heavier bombardment than was delivered against Betio, appeared to doubt that any preliminary bombing, however heavy, could have knocked out altogether the kinds of fortifications and shelters to be found there.

The opinions just cited agreed that a considerably heavier, more accurately placed aerial bombardment would have been necessary for softening the Tarawa defenses. Yet the 78 per cent record achieved by the B-24's in their 50 sorties and the great weight of the naval bombardment could well have encouraged the belief that the ground defenses were sufficiently weakened before the landing craft touched shore. The likelihood of incomplete target intelligence and the difficulty of photographic interpretation go far toward accounting for such disparity between expected and actual results. But the preliminary bombing of invasion beaches is generally of such crucial importance that the maximum concentration of bombing effort consistent with maintaining the necessary element of surprise would seem normally to be justified in all such situations.

SOPAC and SWPA: Thirteenth Air Force

AAF units in the South Pacific Area, notably the 5th and 11th Bombardment Groups (H), were combined as the Thirteenth Air Force under the command of Brig. Gen. Nathan F. Twining on 13 January 1943, with headquarters on Espiritu Santo in the New Hebrides. Both before and immediately after the activation of the new air force, heavies from Espiritu Santo had been ranging out on long, grueling search and antishipping missions by order of Navy area commanders. Protests against this "misuse" of strategic bombers by Maj. Gen. Millard F. Harmon, commanding Army forces in SOPAC, ultimately reached General Arnold, with the result that some slight relief from the search responsibility was arranged. Later in 1943 the Navy began to acquire its own PB4Y's (B-24), with which it flew search missions. General Harmon also raised objections to sending the heavies on low-altitude flights, such as those on 16 September 1942, when five separate strafing attacks were flown by B-17's of the 11th Bombardment Group against dock installations and float planes at Gizo and Rekata Bay in the Solomons.[21] The Thirteenth's record against shipping came in for unfavorable attention, although it was pointed out that such poor results were only to be expected in view of the inadequate numbers of heavy bombers which could be sent out on any given mission. According to AAF doctrine, a flight consisting of at least 9 to 15 heavies was necessary to produce a pattern which would cover such a target as that presented by a moving ship.[22] The best answer to the problem of heavy bomber attacks on enemy shipping was finally provided by the famous "Snooper Squadron" or "Black Cats," a squadron of B-24's equipped with radar for low-altitude night bombing. Established on Guadalcanal in late August 1943, these aircraft functioned with great success against Japanese shipping.[23]

After the establishment of the Americans on Guadalcanal on 7 August 1942, the heavies began staging through Henderson Field under hazardous conditions and sought to aid in beating off and sinking enemy convoys during the long and costly ground struggle for the island. Not until the end of 1942 was Guadalcanal sufficiently secure to permit the basing there of strategic bombers. The XIII Bomber Command could now direct blows at enemy shipping elsewhere, such as at Bougainville, and also at the Munda air base on New Georgia. Late in March 1944 the Thirteenth Air Force passed under the control of SWPA, and during the next month forward elements of the XIII Bomber Command moved to Los Negros in the Admiralties and from there leveled attacks on the great Japanese air and naval installations on Truk atoll, a program which it had begun to carry out late in March from its then more remote bases. Rabaul, however, absorbed more attacks than any other objective, and in the course of them considerable losses were sustained. From March to September 1944, the heavies of both the Thirteenth and Seventh Air Forces, the latter of which was now based on Eniwetok and Kwajalein, struck at enemy strongholds in the Carolines to provide protection for simultaneous advances in northern New Guinea and also for Nimitz's attack on Saipan. Other targets of the Thirteenth were Biak, Noemfoor, Woleai, and Yap. On 15 June 1944 the Thirteenth was assigned to FEAF.[24]

As part of the preparation for the Leyte invasion of October 1944, the Thirteenth neutralized enemy bases in east Borneo. Convoys and defenses were also hit in support of landings at Mindoro, Lingayen,

Corregidor, Palawan, and Mindanao from December 1944 through March 1945. The Thirteenth's heavies delivered a blow against one of the few strategic targets which existed outside the home islands, when, with the aid of the Fifth Air Force, they attacked oil installations at Balikpapan, Borneo, in 5 costly but effective missions in late September and early October 1944, each mission involving from 70 to 100 B-24's.[25] On 8 and 9 January 1945 the B-24's of XIII Bomber Command rendered preliminary support largely by airfield strikes, to the Allied invasion at Lingayen Gulf, Luzon. And on 11 and 12 January, 74 B-24's of the 5th and 307th Groups gave more direct aid to the ground troops by bombing with generally excellent results Japanese bivouac areas and concentrations at San Jose, Del Monte, San Vicente, and Luzon.[26] Throughout the spring of 1945 the air force hit military targets and shipping on and near Borneo, softening the enemy for landings by Allied troops. By August some Thirteenth Air Force units had moved to Okinawa where they were being re-equipped and organized for support work at the time the war ended.[27]

The heavies of XIII Bomber Command, then, performed exclusively as a tactical weapon in SOPAC and later in CINPAC, with the exception of the strikes at oil complexes in Borneo. In addition to its long-range attacks on airdromes, designed both to destroy enemy air power and to shield Allied operations elsewhere, it hit enemy shipping, carried out a great amount of reconnasissance, dropped supplies to friendly troops, and even served as attack planes in a few early missions over Gizo and Rekata Bay. None of these objectives could be considered strategic despite the great distances that had to be covered in reaching them.

SWPA: Fifth Air Force

The Fifth Air Force was constituted at Brisbane, Australia, on 3 September 1942 under the command of Maj. Gen. George C. Kenney. As the American component of the Allied Air Force, MacArthur's air weapon in SWPA, the Fifth was, until the formation of FEAF and of the Twentieth Air Force, the only air force in the Pacific not subject to Navy operational control. Its principal energies were absorbed by the long difficult campaign in New Guinea, by never-ceasing reconnaissance, and by the neutralizing of Rabaul in New Britain. But the Fifth's heavy bombers also functioned effectively, along with mediums and RAAF Beaufighters, in the battle of the Bismarck Sea on 2-3 March 1943.[28] In other antishipping strikes, too, the AAF bombers achieved a reputation for effective work. After November 1943 the chief responsibility for maintaining the neutralization of Rabaul fell to the Thirteenth Air Force, and the Fifth was left free to extend its string of bases in the interior of New Guinea from which the Japanese airfields such as Hollandia could be regularly attacked. And from the Darwin area, the Fifth's bombers ranged out against air, shipping, and even oil targets in Borneo and Java. In July 1944 the Fifth became a part of FEAF, and thereafter it participated with the Thirteenth in preinvasion strikes against such islands as Noemfoor and in softening attacks against the Philippines defenses. During the first half of 1945 it supported mopping-up operations in the Philippines and sent out its B-24's against shipping and shore installations at Hong Kong. Like the Seventh, it was moved to Okinawa in preparation for the great assault on Japan that was rendered unnecessary by the surrender of the enemy on 14 August.[29]

Again, the record of the Fifth Air Force discloses an almost uninterrupted pattern of tactical operations. The foregoing summary, however, does not do justice to a number of support actions carried out by Fifth Air Force heavies during 1943 and 1944. After the landings at Lae early in September 1943, for example, 24 B-24's dropped 96 tons of bombs on gun emplacements, buildings, and trucks around the airdrome. On 22 September the heavies assisted in preparations for the Allied landings at Finschhafen by neutralizing enemy air bases.[30] Evaluation of most of these strikes, however, was rendered most difficult by the heavy jungle.[31] A few months later, in the assault on the Bismarck Archipelago and especially on New Britain, the heavies sometimes participated with mediums in airdrome attacks. On 16 January 1944, to cite an example, 18 B-24's dropped 125 out of 136 x 1,000-pound bombs in the designated target area at Arawe; then B-25's came in to bomb and strafe grounded aircraft from minimum altitude. In these attacks the heavies normally flew at altitudes ranging from 4,5000 to 10,000 feet.[32] A particularly fruitful preinvasion mission against Manus Island was flown on 11 March 1944 by seven B-24's. The heavies not only claimed 198 hits in a troop area with 100-pound phosphorous bombs, but they then strafed the area from treetop level.[33] Another instance of highly accurate preinvasion bombing was executed by 16 B-24's against Noemfoor on 2 July 1944, when the heavies dumped their 250-pound bombs directly on enemy troop positions overlooking the invasion beaches.[34]

The battle for Cape Gloucester on the northwest tip of New Britain, which was preceded by an exceptionally effective preinvasion bombing, provides two clear-cut examples of direct support action by strategic bombers. On 29 December 1943 the Marines called upon the Fifth Air Force for a strike against enemy defenses on Razorback Hill. A bomb line was designated, and 54 B-24's of the 90th, 380th, and 43d Bombardment Groups drenched the area from an altitude of 10,000 feet with 156 tons of 500-pound bombs, none of which fell short of the bomb line. Two circumstances, however, prevented any satisfactory assessment of this bombardment. First, the heavies were followed up immediately by two waves of B-25's and one of B-26's which both bombed and strafed the target area. Second, the Marines delayed their advance on Razorback Hill for nearly six hours, a period which may have allowed the enemy to recover somewhat from the attack, although even then the Japanese put up less opposition than had been expected.[35] On 7 and 10 January 1944 the Marines again called for Fifth Air Force assistance in quelling Japanese troops on Hill 660 near Aogiri Ridge. The response by B-24's of the 43d Bombardment Group resulted on the first occasion in the effective dropping of 216 x 500-pound bombs on the hill position.[36] Such direct-support missions, however, were normally assigned to the A-20's, the fighter-bombers, and sometimes the mediums. Ground force officers not infrequently expressed their appreciation for the effectiveness of these attacks.[37]

CBI: Tenth and Fourteenth Air Forces

Three separate United States air forces operated against the Japanese in Asia, and the general pattern of heavy and very heavy bomber activity in each must be briefly discussed. The Tenth and Fourteenth Air Forces were closely related, both in their origins and in their fields of operations, whereas the B-29's of the XX Bomber Command were not established in the China-Burma-India theater until June 1944 and remained there but a short time.

The Tenth Air Force, activated early in 1942 with headquarters at New Delhi, India, had as its over-all mission the rendering of help to British and Indian forces opposing the Japanese who had invaded Burma in December 1941 and also the maintenance and protection of a supply route into China over the Hump. In its early days the Tenth sought particularly to protect Calcutta and the Assam area from enemy air raids. Soon after its birth, the Tenth sustained a severe blow when its first commander, Maj. Gen. Lewis H. Brereton, and all its heavy bombers were transferred to the Middle East.* Enormous supply difficulties plagued the air force from the outset, and it was some months before the four squadrons of its single heavy bombardment group, the 7th, were fully equipped and ready for action on their bases at Gaya and Pandaveswar in northeastern India. In October 1942 the B-24's of the 7th Group, hoping to knock out power plants and pumping stations, hit the far-off Chinese center of Tientsin by staging through Chengtu. On 5, 9, and 20 November the heavies struck at transportation and industrial targets at Mandalay and Rangoon, and on 28 November and 26 December they again undertook the long flight to Rangoon in order to hit oil refineries there. Such clear-cut strategic missions reveal an interest on the part of the theater commanders in striking at the sources of enemy power.[38]

Throughout 1943, industrial plants, communications centers, and, to a more limited extent, shipping in the vicinity of Rangoon continued

---
* See p. 41 above.

to be favorite targets, even though the latter lay barely within operational range. Oil refineries, oil-storage facilities, railroad yards, and railroad shops were all visited several times. Also, a number of enemy airdromes, such as the large field at Mingaladon, were attacked by the 7th Bombardment Group. Beginning in February, the B-24's added to their repetoire the sowing of magnetic mines in the Rangoon estuary and in other waterways in the vicinity of Moulmein, a profitable operation which continued more or less steadily throughout the remainder of the war. Also, the heavies occasionally cooperated with the mediums in railroad strikes in Burma, and they were further sent out on many largely ineffectual missions against railroad bridges. So low was the score of the heavies against bridges that it soon became clear that such employment was a mistake.[39] The air assault was intensified during November and December by a series of coordinated attacks planned by Maj. Gen. George E. Stratemeyer. These attacks, delivered by the Tenth's mediums and heavies, a small number of RAF bombers, and the 308th Bombardment Squadron on loan from the Fourteenth Air Force, opened inauspiciously on 26 November. Later missions on 27 and 28 November and 1 and 4 December resulted in damage to dock areas at Rangoon and, despite more than moderate losses to enemy interception, considerable destruction of air and rail facilities at Insein, and the sowing of a new crop of mines at Moulmein and Rangoon. Conditions conspired to make impossible any satisfactory estimate of bomb damage or apportionment of credit between the AAF and RAF bombers, the latter of which flew their relatively few missions at night. On 19 and 23 December flights of B-24's hit railroad terminal facilities and recently expanded dock areas at Bangkok.[40]

The pattern of heavy bomber employment in the Tenth Air Force just outlined was not altered significantly during 1944 and 1945. The creation of the Eastern Air Command on 15 December 1943 brought under General Stratemeyer's leadership the Tenth's 237 aircraft, 48 of which were B-24's, and nearly twice that number of RAF planes, including 31 heavies (Liberators). The AAF and RAF heavies and mediums together were organized as the Strategic Air Force, whereas the remainder of the combat aircraft formed the Third Tactical Air Force. The primary responsibility of the Tactical Air Force was to protect the steady stream of Air Transport Command cargo planes as they flew the Hump, especially during January and February 1944 when the Japanese mounted a series of determined air attacks on the route. The Strategic Air Force, for its part, operated against transportation in Burma, the mediums bombing bridges, defiles, and trackage, in which work they were often abetted by fighter-bombers on the prowl for locomotives and rolling stock. The heavies, ranging farther out, searched for enemy shipping, mined waterways, and struck at port installations, rail centers, and industrial targets like the refineries at Yenangyaung.[41] The Tenth also figured importantly in the repulse of the Japanese ground offensive of February 1944, largely by supplying encircled troops from the air. The strategic air assault greatly limited Japanese use of Rangoon and even of Bangkok as ports of entry, and the former city was evacuated by 2 May 1945. Shortly thereafter, because of the lessening of the Japanese threat from Burma, the Tenth Air Force was redeployed to China where, in July 1945, its headquarters was combined with that of the Fourteenth Air Force. The new operational area assigned to the Tenth was east China south of the 27th parallel where, at about the time of the Japanese surrender, it was to have begun functioning against the home islands.[42]

With the exception of the costly and generally unsuccessful bridge-busting missions, the Tenth Air Force combat record reveals no significant diversions of heavy bombers from strategic to tactical objectives. Such strategic targets as were accessible in the theater—docks, port facilities, shipping, communications centers, railroad shops, and refineries—were barred from the beginning, and the remaining energies of the 7th Bombardment Group were expended in long-range reconnaissance over the Andaman Sea, airfield strikes, supply drops, mine-sowing, and, not infrequently, trucking flights over the Hump. Most of the missions in this last group were utility rather than clear-cut tactical operations.

The limited heavy bomber activities on the part of Brig. Gen. Claire L. Chennault's Fourteenth Air Force may be very briefly summarized. The Fourteenth was not activated until 10 March 1943. Its immediate predecessor was the China Air Task Force, a Tenth Air Force detachment which operated largely out of the Kunming area, but ultimately it sprang from the famous American Volunteer Group, which, from December 1941 to July 1942, protected the Kunming air-supply terminal and sought to deny the Japanese entrance into Yunnan from the southwest. The fact that the Fourteenth had to subsist entirely on supplies flown over the Hump gravely impaired its activities, especially those of the heavy bombers, which had to haul much of their own gasoline and other supplies. Heavy bomber operations in the new air force were initiated on 4 May 1943 when 18 B-24's pounded port facilities, an oil refinery, and an air base on the island of Hainan. On 9 May B-24's and B-25's cooperated in a successful strike on an airfield at Canton. During the summer the heavies and mediums concentrated on merchant shipping, and in the autumn Formosa was attacked and many enemy aircraft destroyed on the ground. In May, Japanese troops pressing up the Yangtze River toward Chungking, the provisional capital of China, were bombed by B-24's in attacks that may well have contributed to the enemy withdrawal. During another offensive near Changsha, the heavies rendered some slight aid by hitting enemy fighter bases. Again, one of the Fourteenth's heavy bomber squadrons was sent against Japanese supply lines during the futile attempt on the part of Chinese and American troops to drive across the Salween River in June 1944.[43]

The Japanese began closing in on American forward air bases later in 1944, but as the tide turned against them in Burma and elsewhere, they were slowly forced back to the Canton and Hankow areas. In support of the assault on the Philippines in October 1944 the Fourteenth struck Formosa and air installations on the China coast. But later, because Allied bomber bases in the Philippines were better placed than the few mainland bases for antishipping sweeps along the coast and because of the loss of advanced bases to the Japanese offensive, the Fourteenth was set to work on railroad systems, steel plants, and other important targets in north China. Enemy efforts to reach Hsian, from which these attacks were mounted, failed partly because of Fourteenth Air Force cooperation with Chinese ground troops. After the establishment in July 1945 of the Tenth Air Force on its old eastern bases, the Fourteenth was directed to continue its campaign against transportation and other objectives useful to the Japanese in north China.[44]

Twentieth Air Force

Because XX Bomber Command was equipped with the hastily perfected B-29 and organized exclusively for strategic bombing, its combat record in the Far East and the Pacific would seem to be irrelevant to the present study. B-29's, however, were used to a minor extent in neutralizing air bases on Iwo Jima and were even diverted from strategic missions to hit kamikaze fields on Kyushu. Furthermore, a brief discussion of B-29 operations in World War II will serve as background for an understanding of B-29 employment in the Korean conflict.

The first raid on the Japanese home islands since General Doolittle's famous attack of April 1942 (with the exception of the Eleventh Air Force missions to the Kurils) was flown on 15 June 1944 by China-based B-29's of XX Bomber Command. The series of attacks thus initiated was so limited by the supply bottleneck, however, that only 800 tons of bombs could be delivered against Japanese industrial targets before April 1945, when the very heavy bombers were transferred to Marianas bases. It was from these hurriedly constructed bases on the newly-won islands of Saipan, Guam, and Tinian that XXI Bomber Command had begun launching attacks on 24 November 1944. With a steadily increasing tempo, the big bombers hit Japan throughout the remainder of the war. Spectacular incendiary raids were made on Tokyo, Osaka, Kobe, and Nagoya beginning in February 1945, and all important industrial centers within range were subjected to precision bombing. Also, the aerial mining of Japanese waters was carried out vigorously. The few departures from this strategic program may be quickly indicated. The XXI Bomber Command, during the last month of 1944 and the first two months of 1945, devoted perhaps 10 per cent of its bomb tonnage to the Iwo Jima bases from which the Japanese were striking at the Marianas and interfering with B-29 operations. Even these attacks, it was learned later, were insufficient to soften the island for the amphibious invasion. Again, just before the Okinawa landings in April 1945, the XXI Bomber Command hit air bases on Kyushu,, and XX Bomber Command attacked similar installations in northern Formosa. The sowing of mines, although largely a strategic effort to blockade Japan, indirectly figured as a part of the invasion support provided by the B-29's.[45]

Such counter-air strikes by the Twentieth Air Force were minor compared with the bombing of the kamikaze bases in Kyushu during the period 17 April-11 May 1945. Suicide pilots, who began flying their attacks in October 1944, were sinking and severely damaging naval vessels at a disastrous rate. In all, some 2,550 suicide sorties were flown, of which approximately 475 succeeded in sinking or damaging their objectives. The loss by sinking of 45 ships, many of them destroyers, and the damaging of many scores of other vessels, created a major emergency. Consequently, the B-29's were ordered to shift their sights from strategic targets in and around the industrial centers to the air bases on Kyushu. Some 2,000 B-29 sorties were thus diverted and dropped their great weight of bombs on the kamikaze fields. The effectiveness of their efforts was soon evident in the falling off of suicide missions. No fewer than 22 B-29's were lost in this operation, but even this cost was not excessive in view of the threat posed by a force of 5,000 suicide pilots.[46]

Thus the B-29's in the Pacific war, apart from counter-air missions of a rather special type, functioned as a purely strategic air weapon. Out of a total of 160,800 tons of bombs dropped on the Japanese home islands, the B-29's accounted for 92 per cent. By far the major portion of this weight fell in the area bombing of cities, and the remainder was distributed among aircraft factories, oil refineries, coke plants, arsenals, and miscellaneous industries. The total of 12,054 mines which were sown proved astonishingly successful in sinking enemy merchant shipping. Projected programs of bombing transportation centers and electric power plants were never put into effect because the Japanese surrender followed hard on the dropping by B-29's of the first two atom bombs on 6 and 9 August 1945.[47]

To the extent that strategic objectives were accessible to the three air forces in the CBI, heavy bomber activities there differed from those in the Pacific areas to the east. It is true that, apart from attacking rail centers, refineries, port facilities, and industries at such cities as Rangoon, and sowing mines, the heavy bombers of the Tenth Air Force searched for enemy shipping and pounded Japanese air bases, just as did the heavies of the Fifth, Seventh, and Thirteenth Air Forces. The very few B-24's of the Fourteenth Air Force also flew occasional strategic missions, especially during the last months of the war when steel plants in Manchuria came under attack. Mine-sowing and antishipping strikes were assigned to the heavies in China, and a handful of B-24's bombed enemy troops and supply lines during the Japanese advance toward Chungking in mid-1944. The Twentieth Air Force, operating from the CBI for but a few months, departed from its strategic mission only long enough to carry out important counter-air attacks. Despite the tactical nature of a number of the missions just summarized, it is obvious that strategic bombers of these air forces operated more strictly in conformity with standard employment doctrine than could the heavies in the several Pacific theaters. Also to be observed is that, aside from the participation of the XIII Bomber Command in ground fighting, especially on Luzon, no important instances of the use of heavy bombers in close support over a battlefield seem to be on record.[48]

* * * * * *

It has been observed that a significant difference between aerial warfare in the ETO and in the war against Japan is that American airmen in Europe were able to profit from the accumulated combat experience of the RAF, whereas in the Pacific the Americans were pioneers in the solution of unprecedented problems. The experience gained in Europe was scarcely applicable to the island-hopping Pacific war. It was even found that the theory that an enemy surface attack could be effectively countered by land-based bombers--a basic concept of long standing in national defense plans--was not always realistic in the face of conditions under which the fighting in the Pacific developed. The well-equipped permanent bases necessary for the efficient and sustained operation of heavy bombers were not available to the Army air arm where they were needed nor could they be constructed until after many long months of the war had passed. The heavies were heavily handicapped by the primitive island airstrips from which they were all toooften forced to work.[49]

Again, the virtually complete absence of strategic targets in the Pacific told against the record of the B-17's and B-24's. Of all the tactical targets, enemy shipping enjoyed the highest priority, yet it was precisely against moving ships that the heavy bombers were least effective. It is true that Navy operational control and insufficient numbers of bombers for formation bombing were probably in large part responsible for this failure. A considerable improvement in accuracy was effected as the war progressed by drastically reducing the altitude of attack and by the use of airborne radar equipment.[50]

But if the heavies were by no means as successful in hitting moving ships as the Navy's SBD and TBF combination or as B-25's,[51] they were indispensable in conducting long-range sea search, as is evidenced by the Navy's procurement of B-24's for just this purpose. And despite the opinion of experts that the vast majority of targets in the Pacific were best suited to tactical or medium bombers, the distances to be flown in reaching these objectives more often than not greatly exceeded the operating range of the B-25's and B-26's.[52] Thus the heavies, mainly the B-24's, performed much of the airstrip bombing because they were the only air weapon in the theater with the necessary range. The neutralizing of enemy air bases, usually for the purpose of isolating a battlefield on one of the contested islands, was undoubtedly the most valuable single contribution of the heavies to the Pacific war, although their work in occasional close-support situations and in bombing strategic targets in Asia was also of significance.

AHS-88

Chapter VI
THE KOREAN CONFLICT, 1950-1951

A satisfactory analysis of almost any aspect of the Korean war is a task of peculiar difficulty. At the time of writing, the conflict was still in progress and neither enemy records nor key military personnel were available for correcting tentative assessments of operations. Apart from this obvious handicap are those arising from the unparalleled restrictions imposed upon the combatants. The American forces fighting there were only one component, although by far the most important, of the United Nations armies, and thus they were at least theoretically subject to the direction of the United Nations organization. Also, this conflict was technically a "police action," the delicate objective of which was to enforce a United Nations decree in the interests of world peace without touching off a world-wide conflagration. In the nature of things, then, the Korean war was a limited operation into which the United States and China, at least, dared not throw the full weight of their armed might.

The first 18 months of the war fall conveniently into 5 phases. The initial phase opened on Sunday, 25 June 1950, when North Korean troops without warning drove across the 38th parallel separating North and South Korea. The impetus of this advance pushed the inadequately prepared south Koreans and hastily assembled Americans far down the peninsula into the tiny defense perimeter in the southeast around Taegu and the port of Pusan.

There the United Nations held and built up their forces until, beginning 15 September, they opened the second round by breaking the enemy ring and pushing the Communists rapidly to the north. As a result of the amphibious landings at Inchon, the U.N. forces were able to sweep up to the 38th parallel and then beyond to press the enemy in a narrow strip along the Manchurian border by mid-November. The third phase began with the appearance in battle of great numbers of well-equipped Chinese Communist troops, who on 26 November succeeded in turning back the United Nations and forcing a retreat which finally halted well below the 38th parallel and the South Korean capital of Seoul. The six months of bitter fighting of the fourth phase brought the United Nations again up to the parallel at most points. There the combatants were still facing each other when the truce talks began at Kaesong early in July 1951. The fifth phase of the war, which carried through the end of the year and beyond, witnessed local engagements of varying frequency and savagery, and a considerable development of the air war.

The aerial resources, and particularly the strategic bombers, available to the United Nations forces during the first 18 months may be quickly indicated. Close at hand were the Fifth Air Force based in Japan, and the Twentieth Air Force based on Guam and Okinawa. The Twentieth Air Force, however, was represented only by the 19th Bombardment Group (M) with its 27 B-29's. The B-29, which in 1949 had been redesignated a medium bomber,* was the only strategic bomber to be made available to

---

*See p. 4 above.

FEAF for combat duty. Medium bomber strength was promptly augmented by the arrival during the second week of July of the 22d and 92d Bombardment Groups (M), and, early in August, of the 98th and 307th Groups. The speedy deployment of the two last-named groups in battle-ready condition from scattered bases in the United States was an impressive indication of the efficiency of the newest of the armed services. The successes of the United Nations forces during the second phase of the war led to the release on 22 October 1950 of the 22d and 92d Groups from combat service, and they were not recalled to the theater of operations. After October 1950 FEAF commanded only three groups of medium bombers. The FEAF Bomber Command (Provisional) was organized at Yokota on 8 July 1950 to provide operational control of the strategic bombers.[1]

The present concern is with the ways in which the B-29's were employed during the period from 25 June 1950 through 31 December 1951 and with their effectiveness in carrying out tactical tasks. That the peculiar conditions governing the Korean conflict had a profound bearing on the combat mission of the B-29's will become apparent in the review of medium bomber activities which follows. It is convenient to describe such operations under two heads: first, Phase I of the war (25 June-30 September 1950), during which period the United Nations forces were fighting desperately for their existence in Korea; and, second, Phases II-V (1 October 1950 through 31 December 1951), the period which saw the defeat of the North Koreans, the entrance of the Chinese in the war, and the beginnings of the long stalemate.

Phase I: 25 June—30 September 1950

So sudden was the North Korean onslaught of 25 June that there was no time to observe the refinements of military doctrine. The enemy had to be hit at once with every available weapon. In this emergency the B-29's of the 19th Bombardment Group flew from their island bases more than 1,000 miles to the south and joined the fighters and other tactical aircraft of the Fifth Air Force in battlefield action. On 28 June, 4 B-29's released 31 tons of bombs on a rail bridge and on front-line targets of opportunity, with emphasis on tanks, trucks, and supply columns. Kimpo airfield and the railroad station at Seoul, now in enemy hands, received the attention of eight mediums the next day. From 8 to 16 sorties were flown on 30 June and 1, 2, 5, and 6 July against airfields, bridges, troop concentrations, and other battle-area objectives. Tactical targets such as these had never been contemplated by the designers of the B-29, nor had close-in work been assigned to any unit of the Twentieth Air Force during World War II. Yet the big planes suffered no combat losses during these early Korean raids, and their crews could occasionally announce good results.[2] One report has it that some strafing passes were made by B-29's at treetop level, but such attacks must have been rare.[3]

The first clear-cut strategic attack was made on 7 July against port facilities at Wonsan and a nitrogen fertilizer plant and the Rising Sun Refinery in the same vicinity. On these targets 11 B-29's dropped 88 tons of bombs and again escaped without loss. On the next day, the mediums went back to communications and tactical targets, 10 of them hitting bridges at the battle front and 8 more the Chinnampo dock area. On 9 July the critical ground situation again required that distant marshalling-yard missions be canceled in favor of the bombing of important bridges 25 to 30 miles behind the front lines.[4] Very similar missions were flown nearly every day throughout the remainder of the month. On the 12th, aircraft of the newly arrived 92d Bombardment Group entered the conflict, and on the next day when the 22d Group also joined the battle, the number of effective sorties rose sharply to 55. Some B-29's flew reconnaissance and leaflet-dropping missions, but the bulk of the mediums' effort was directed toward the bombing of communications within or close to the battle area. Occasionally, however, cloud cover forced the bombers to seek targets north of the 38th parallel. On the 16th, 3 aircraft released on the friendly town of Andong instead of the assigned target at the Tanyang, killing 22 South Koreans and wounding 8 others.[5]

There is no doubt that during the month of July the mediums rendered valuable assistance to the tactical planes of the Fifth Air Force in their great effort to slow the North Korean advance. The brief respite thus gained permitted United Nations forces to organize their lines around Pusan.[6] FEAF Bomber Command leaders were fully cognizant of the desperate ground plight, and in accordance with the long-established doctrine of flexibility, they were eager that their B-29's whenever feasible, provide direct aid to the hard-pressed troops. At the same time, these leaders were painfully aware that the strength of the Bomber Command was not being applied to best advantage. The basic difficulty lay in the fact that FEAF was not properly represented in the Far East Command and that, consequently, target selection and the consignment of strategic aircraft to support of the Eighth Army were in the hands of officers with little experience with or understanding of air power. On one occasion the GHQ Target Analysis Group ordered a bomber attack on two highway and rail bridges which had never been built. The result of this sort of control was to keep the mediums fully occupied with battlefield and random communications targets, thus preventing them from embarking on a systematic interdiction campaign, which, as air officers had learned in World War II, would be in all probability the most effective aid which they could render the front-line troops.[7]

It is true that a directive of 11 July 1950 specified that FEAF Bomber Command should attack communications north of the 38th parallel on first priority, but an amendment of a few days later directed that close-support operations beyond the capabilities of the Fifth Air Force should be performed by the B-29's and that such work should take precedence over all other missions.[8] In actual practice, virtually 75 per cent of the medium bomber effort during June and July was absorbed by FEAF calls for tactical missions. A somewhat later directive set forth the official definition of three types of medium bomber missions: 1) strategic, designed to destroy or neutralize the enemy's capacity or will to wage war through attacks on selected targets within his national structure; 2) close-support, normally flown under the direction of a tactical controller, either ground or air, in support of front-line troops; and 3) interdiction, planned to disrupt the flow of enemy materiel or personnel to the front-line battle zone.[9] The objectives assigned to the B-29's during June and July fell mostly into the two last-named categories.

Not until the end of July was FEAF able, as a result of General Stratemeyer's vigorous objections, to exert more control over target selection and the Bomber Command placed in a position to develop an interdiction and a strategic program. On 25 July, for example, two medium groups were released from calls for close support to permit their initiating a carefully planned interdiction program. As the following survey suggests, these strikes were directed chiefly against railroad bridges and communications centers.

The interdiction plan that was carried out was a thorough one. On one day, a B-29 strike would fall on cities and towns across Korea from Pyongyang to Wonsan. Below this line, B-26 light bombers would bomb towns like Sariwon and Kosong, and fighters would concentrate on still more southerly objectives. The next day, the B-29's would hit farther to the north, the B-26's would work over the towns already struck the day before by the B-29's, and the fighters would seek to intensify the destruction left the day before by the light bombers.[10] A study of B-29 operations during August and the first half of September shows that combat strikes were made on two out of every three days during this period. A far larger share of the effort was expended on communications targets than during June and July, although tactical support missions continued to be flown. Moreover, sizeable forces were sent out on mapping and reconnaissance flights. On a typical day, such as 6 September, 25 B-29's attacked the railroad yards at Pyongyang, 18 more hit selected railroad and highway bridges in North Korea, and 3 aircraft conducted mapping and surveillance missions. Also, beginning 1 September, as many as 40 to 50 B-29's were held in reserve for close-in strikes in direct aid of United Nations forces in the Pusan beachhead.[11]

Although no full evaluation of the aerial interdiction program during these most critical days and of the part in this program played by the FEAF Bomber Command would be possible until the war was over, all available evidence indicated that, starved of munitions and supplies by the aerial blockade, the North Korean armies hammering at the Pusan perimeter had become largely ineffective by early September.[12]

Strategic objectives in Korea were by no means numerous. From the beginning, air officers recognized that the primary contribution of air power in Korea would be tactical. Nevertheless, such industries basic to the North Korean war effort as existed were carefully studied and brought under systematic attack, principally by the B-29's. The first undoubtedly strategic missions against a refinery and munitions works at Wonsan and Hungnam on 13 July have already been mentioned. Early in August the target system outlined by FEAF comprised arsenals, railroad shops, yards, bridges, and the like at Pyongyang, the capital of North Korea; the harbor, submarine base, and two iron works at Chongjin; an oil refinery, locomotive shops, and naval base at Wonsan; explosives plants at Hungnam; and a chemical plant at Rashin, very near the northern border. This list of targets was extended on 15 August by the addition of factories and marshalling yards at Chinnampo, Songjin, Hamhung, and Haeju. The efforts of two B-29 groups were devoted to these strategic targets for approximately five weeks, at the end of which period, on 12 September, General Stratemeyer could announce that nearly all had been 50 to 95 per cent destroyed. The very rapid countermarch of the United Nations forces out of their Pusan beachhead during the latter part of September resulted in JCS directive on the 26th of the month that strategic missions be canceled and all elements of the Air Force concentrate for the time being on tactical operations.[13]

The battlefield targets assigned to FEAF Bomber Command during August and September were much the same as those flown in July. On 9 September, for example, 49 B-29's attacked 9 villages immediately behind the battle lines in response to a call for close support of ground troops. On other days, highways and rail lines in the battle zone were cut at critical chokepoints, flare missions were flown in conjunction with tactical bombers, and troops and materiel concentrations were bombed. The B-29's performing such missions operated under the direction of the Joint Operations Center, the same headquarters which handled the close-in activities of Fifth Air Force planes. In the meantime, the interdiction and strategic campaigns were also going on, and individual aircraft flew leaflet and reconnaissance missions.[14]

The most spectacular of all the B-29 tactical operations was the saturation bombing of an enemy-held area near Waegwan on 16 August. Only two days before, Maj. Gen. Emmett O'Donnell, Jr., commanding FEAF Bomber Command (Prov.), had set forth Air Force requirements for area-bombing missions in support of friendly forces. The most important of these conditions were as follows: sufficient ceiling for visual bombing, a clearly recognizable topographical feature which could serve as a marker for the bomb line, adequate prestrike photographic coverage, a target area

Finally, FEAF recommended to the Commander in Chief, Far East that no more B-29 carpet-bombing missions of this type be attempted in the future.[17] Several requests for such efforts were later rejected by FEAF Bomber Command because of the impossibly great size of the designated target areas.[18]

The emphasis in B-29 operations during the first months of the Korean war, then, shifted rather sharply from close-support to interdiction and strategic missions, despite the tactical bombing at Waegwan in August. This shift is clearly reflected in the monthly tabulation of sorties flown by FEAF Bomber Command which is reproduced below:[19]

Period	Close Support	Interdiction	Strategic	Other
25-30 June 1950	408	59	0	100
1-31 July	4,635	1,023	56	1,827
1-31 August	7,397	2,963	539	4,582
1-30 September	5,969	3,818	158	5,382

During the first days of the conflict, close support outnumbered interdiction sorties 7 to 1 and no strategic missions at all were flown. During July the rate of close support to interdiction was more than 4 to 1. The peak of B-29 operations was reached in August when interdiction and strategic sorties together totaled somewhat less than one-half the number of direct-support sorties, and in September the interdiction and strategic activity grew proportionately larger, despite the fact that the Bomber Command had by then run short of strategic targets.

no wider than five miles, and, finally, assurance that the designated area contained at least two enemy divisions which were on the point of delivering an attack. On 15 August an area near Waegwan in which there were thought to be perhaps 40,000 enemy troops bent on crossing the Naktong River for an attack on the U.S. 1st Cavalry Division front was singled out for a B-29 carpet-bombing mission. General O'Donnell was aware that effective saturation of an area 3.5 by 7.5 miles could scarcely be achieved by the 12 squadrons of mediums available for the operation, but the attack was carried out on the 16th. Beginning at noon, 98 B-29's streamed over the target area, dropping 3,084 x 500-pound and 150 x 1,000-pound general-purpose bombs. Three more B-29's flew reconnaissance and one dropped warning leaflets. Inasmuch as the Naktong River separated the enemy's territory from friendly troops, the bombardiers were able to avoid bombing short and thus endangering their comrades. Very light and ineffectual antiaircraft fire was encountered, and the mediums released their 839 tons and returned to their bases without suffering any losses.[15]

Because there was no advance on the part of United Nations troops, an adequate assessment of the Waegwan bombing was never made. It is worth noting, however, that General O'Donnell, on the basis of a personal reconnaissance of the area before the bombing, was skeptical that it contained any sizeable enemy forces.[16] The official opinion of FEAF was that the area was entirely too large for the bomber force available and that the B-29's could have been far more effectively employed against interdiction or strategic targets. At the same time, the possibility that the bombing contributed to the morale of friendly troops was admitted.

Phases II-V: 1 October 1950--31 December 1951

During this 15-month period, the medium bombers continued for the most part to subsist on a diet of close-support and interdiction targets. The natural strategic objectives after November 1950, when the Soviet-supported Chinese poured across the border of North Korea to initiate what was, in fact, a new war, were the Manchurian supply centers and assembly areas, but such targets had to be held inviolate for political reasons.[20]

The volume and character of the interdiction and close-support missions of the B-29's from October onward may be quickly indicated. Although a high level of medium bomber activity continued through the first week of October 1950, 286 sorties divided evenly between interdiction and tactical strikes being flown during that period, a slackening in effort is to be noted immediately thereafter. The reasons are not far to seek. In step with the rapid advance of the ground forces, the bomb line moved steadily to the north, thus limiting FEAF Bomber Command operations to an ever-decreasing section of North Korea. So speedy was the advance that the armed-reconnaissance objectives of one day sometimes became the close-support targets of the next. Also it was during this week, on 3 October, that General O'Donnell officially announced the end of the strategic air campaign.[21]

Throughout the remainder of the month, the mediums successfully hit an arsenal at Kanni, a military training center at Hungnam, a warehouse at Songjin, and an ammunition storage area at Namgong-ni, north of Pyongyang. During the week of 8 to 14 October, a tactical strike was made on movements of troops and supplies southeast of Antung, Manchuria. The bulk of the effort, however, was directed against some 23 bridges and other key points on 3 railroads and highways in northwest Korea and on the northeast coast between Tanchon and Chongjin. Often, delayed-action bombs were released on the targets. Of the 23 bridges on the interdiction list, 20 were destroyed or rendered unusable. The continuing success of the ground forces led to the release on 22 October of the 22d and 92d Groups of mediums. The elimination of many targets brought about a sharp reduction in medium bomber sorties to a token effort of 12 per day, exclusive of leaflet dropping and reconnaissance, during the period 21 to 24 October. From 25 October through the end of the month, the Bomber Command stood down. Operations were resumed in November, however, when North Korean resistance increased, the primary effort being aimed at the isolation of battle areas and attacks with incendiary bombs against key supply and communications centers, such as Chongjin, Sinchon, and Changjon. The heaviest of these assaults hit Hoeryong. International bridges, like the one at Sinuiju, were also bombed.[22] The Fifth Air Force bore the brunt of the close-in tactical work during the period when the Chinese attempted to close a trap on the 1st Cavalry Division. For example, using MPQ-2 radar equipment night flying B-26's of the 3d Bombardment Group (L) hit front-line targets within 1,000 yards of I Corps troops.[23]

The December missions were mainly directed against such communications centers as the Pyongyang marshalling yards and also against various supply bases. B-29's were further used for propaganda leaflet drops and for surveillance and mapping operations. The first drop of tarzon bombs, the targets, and the usual close-support attacks were flown by an average of three B-29's nightly.[28]

Of particular importance was the appearance during September of Russian fighter planes, the MIG-15's, over North Korea. On 26 September, Lt. Gen. Otto P. Weyland, FEAF commander, notified General Vandenberg that because of this new development, unescorted B-29 missions would no longer be practicable. This fear was well founded, for the next month witnessed the first significant combat losses suffered by the B-29's. During the period 21-27 October, violent air battles were waged between the MIG-15's and the B-29's and their escorts, especially the F-84's and F-86's. No fewer than 5 B-29's were lost, and 8 more were badly damaged. In the whole course of the Korean war up to this point, only 6 B-29's had been shot down by enemy aircraft. The October losses prompted FEAF Bomber Command to concentrate more than before on night attacks when hitting targets which were located in sensitive areas, a restriction that remained in force through the end of the year.[29]

The October and November schedule of interdiction and close-support targets was much the same as that of preceding months. Temporary bridges erected by the enemy to replace critical crossings were repeatedly bombed, as were airdromes and marshalling yards. Airfields were given the highest priority at this time, but when all designated airfields had been at least temporarily put out of service, the B-29's increased their strikes at marshalling yards. A great many of these missions were flown at night with radar aids, and the three to four close-support sorties that were sent out nightly also released on radar very often. Proximity-fuzed air-bursting bombs came to be used in drops on front-line troops, apparently

	Sorties	Tonnage
Bypass bridge	6	36
Railroad bridges (Yonghung)	7	52
Ammunition and supply dump	1	3
Hungnam barracks area	1	10

The 53 close-support sorties, comprising 36 per cent of total activity, were directed mainly against troop concentrations and villages harboring troops. The radar-controlled drops enumerated in the above table were regarded as especially worth while by the ground forces. One could scarcely classify any of these missions as strategic. FEAF sources list no strategic attacks by the Bomber Command subsequent to September 1950.

Throughout the second half of 1951, the slowly decreasing numbers of B-29 sorties were devoted to close support and the various kinds of interdiction objectives in roughly the same proportion as had been maintained in June. There were, however, shifts in emphasis. In July, FEAF Bomber Command sent its mediums chiefly against marshalling yards, supply bases, and rail systems. Many of these attacks were guided by shoran equipment. Night close-support attacks aided by MPQ-2 radar on troops in the battle zone were carried on by at least two B-29's each night, but daytime bombing assaults were also made on front-line targets, such as an attack of 12-14 July, which was delivered by 11 planes. In August the same kinds of targets were struck, the principal innovation being the bombing on the 25th of railroad yards at Rashin, theretofore regarded as off limits because of its proximity to the Manchurian border. In September, marshalling yards, airfields, and bridges, with emphasis on four key crossings at Pyongyang, Sinanju, Sunchen, and Songchon, constituted the chief interdiction

12,000-pound remotely controlled missiles, occurred in December with disappointing results. A request originating with X Corps headquarters was made of FEAF Bomber Command to bomb three towns along the front on 7 December. Since the mission seemed feasible to air officers, preparations were made for its execution, but improvement in the ground situation led to the cancellation of the request. Three other requests on 27 December for area bombing of troop concentrations between Seoul and Chorwon were rejected, however, because of the higher priority enjoyed by built-up areas near enemy lines and also because the specified objectives were too large for satisfactory bomb coverage. One area, for example, was 14 square miles in extent. Since it was considered that 25 to 30 B-29's were required effectually to saturate a single square mile of territory, the now slender resources of the Bomber Command did not permit undertaking such great tasks.[24]

The opening of the new year saw a continuation of these types of medium bomber employment although innovation came about from time to time. On 5 February 1951 a new policy went into effect which restricted close-in interdiction targets to Fifth Air Force tactical planes. The policy was dictated by a desire to conserve the fighter escort now felt necessary for B-29's flying over the battle zone. But on 1 March, B-29's returned to escorted bridge-busting missions because of the lack of success experienced by the Fifth Air Force in such efforts. At the same time, FEAF Bomber Command was ranging out against communications, especially bridges, in northern and eastern Korea, far beyond the front lines. Another development of interest here was the effort made on 17 February 1951 by the FEAF Evaluation Division to regularize the reporting and assessing of medium bomber strikes. Bombing results were thereafter to be classified as excellent, good, fair, or poor. Moreover, the classification was not to be made solely on the basis of the concentration of bomb bursts around predetermined aiming points. Rather, over-all effectiveness, such as visible damage to enemy installations or demoralization of troops, was also to be taken into account. Finally, on 23 February, 2 B-29's using MPQ-2 radar bombed a highway bridge northeast of Seoul. Results on the first run were poor, but excellent on the second. During the month of February, on missions of all types, an average of approximately 181 effective sorties were flown per week. The weekly bomb tonnage totaled nearly 1,445 tons, an average of 8 tons per bomber.[25]

The number of weekly sorties diminished in March to an average of 163, in June to 140, in September to no more than 115, and in December 1951 to approximately 85.[26] That the kinds of targets attacked by the mediums did not represent any basic change may be illustrated from recapitulation of the 19th Bombardment Wing's operations for the month of July 1951:[27]

	Number of Sorties	Bomb Tonnage
Close support (AN-MPQ-2 missions)	53	507
Airfields (Hwangju, Onjong-ni, etc.)	30	215
Marshalling yards (Chinnampo, Hungnam, etc.)	21	172
Communications and supply centers (Hamhung, etc.)	26	208

with good results. No B-29's seem to have been lost to enemy aircraft during November, but one was downed by ground fire and another was recorded as having been lost to enemy action, "cause unknown." Shoran equipment was proving especially useful in locating targets, both at night and in bad visibility in daytime, and an effort was made to install such equipment in all B-29's.[30]

In December there were again no medium bomber losses, although an increase in enemy fighter strength was noted. Enemy airfields were still first-priority targets, but less effort was needed to keep them out of service. With the exception of a routine assignment of two B-29's nightly to airfield neutralization and of three to close support, the principal effort was against key railroad crossings. The continued lull in the ground battle resulted in very few calls for close-in air support.[31]

A fuller understanding of the complex work of the B-29's during 1951 may, perhaps, be conveyed by a brief description of an actual operations order issued by FEAF to its Bomber Command in which the responsibilities of the latter for one day were set forth. The directive chosen for this purpose is Operations Order No. 204-21, wherein mission No. 462, flown 30 June 1951, was fully outlined.

The mission assigned to the medium bombers for 30 June was a dual one: to destroy specified targets in North Korea and also provide close support to ground forces. The 19th Bombardment Group was ordered to send 6 B-29's, each loaded with 7.5 tons of 100-pound general-purpose bombs, to bomb Pyongyang East airfield from 22,000 feet at daylight. The aircraft were to penetrate North Korea at Yosu and pick up their fighter escort at

Singosan while flying at an altitude of 23,000 feet. After bombs-away the B-29's were to leave Korea at Mokpo and return to their base on Okinawa. Three other mediums were to attack the north-south runway of an airfield at Onjong-ni, also by day, from an altitude of 17,000 feet. The point of entry, the place of rendezvous with escort fighters, the "coast-out," and the bomb loads and fuzings were specified. Two other aircraft of the 19th Group were ordered to fly individual close support at night with the aid of their AN-MPQ-2 equipment. They were to enter Korea at Yosu and continue to the control point at Seoul, where specific targets would be assigned. One B-29 of the 98th Bombardment Wing was to conduct a shoran-guided attack on a railroad bridge from 25,000 feet and to photograph the target both before and after the 8 bomb runs it was to make. Finally, the 91st Strategic Reconnaissance Squadron was to fly a number of photographic missions.[32]

The execution of this particular mission, though not altogether satisfactory, was probably typical of the B-29 operations of this period. Pyongyang East airfield and the airfield at Onjong-ni were both hit according to plan although at the former a moderate amount of inaccurate flak was thrown up. The aircrews doubted that the enemy could be using gun-laying radar. One aircraft, because of engine failure, bombed a secondary target, a marshalling yard at Kowon, and then landed at Itazuke. The night attacks were hampered by a technical malfunction; the signals emitted by the ground beacons were not properly received by the airborne equipment. Nevertheless, one of the two aircraft assigned to close support bombed an enemy troop area from 17,500 feet by following directions given by VHF ground control. The other B-29, because of failure even to pick up the signal of the VHF ground station, dropped on a last-resort target. The single bomber dispatched against the railroad bridge released with the assistance of shoran even though visual conditions prevailed. The bombing of the Pyongyang air base, as assessed by photographic interpreters, was considered excellent, since the bombs walked across the runway within 200 feet of the aiming point. The one plane which hit a secondary target at Kowon achieved only fair results, since the bursts were short and to one side of the trackage. At Onjong-ni the bombing was excellent. Of the two mediums flying close support, one was directed to drop on the Hungnam barracks area, and the other released over territory thought to contain enemy troops. The results of these close-support sorties could not be observed—a common fate of such operations.[33]

. . . .

During the period of 25 June 1950 through 31 December 1951, the mediums of FEAF Bomber Command carried out strategic, interdiction, and close-support functions. Strategic work, for which the B-29 was specifically designed, consumed a very small proportion of the total bomb expenditure, for reasons already given. Virtually all installations of great strategic significance to the North Koreans were destroyed within the first three months of the war although constant surveillance was necessary to detect signs of renewed activity and of the development of other installations.

Some confusion tended to creep into the classification of interdiction and close-support targets. A directive of 18 July 1950, already quoted, defined an interdiction mission as one which had as its purpose the disrupting of the flow of enemy materiel or personnel to the front lines, whereas a close-support mission was merely said to be an attack made under the direction of a tactical controller in support of front-line troops. In Korea, control was generally exercised by tactical air control parties, the forward elements of the Tactical Air Control Center. One of the main differences was that the interdiction mission was preplanned, but the close-support attack was one arranged on very short notice. Confusion arose, however, when B-29's in close support were sent against rail lines, bridges, highways, and other targets, the destruction of which would certainly interdict enemy movements. On other occasions, the Tactical Air Control Center sent the mediums against such unambiguous close-support objectives as troop concentrations, supply columns, enemy strongpoints, and the like.

A fully satisfactory evaluation of the tactical activities of FEAF Bomber Command, with particular reference to interdiction and close support, during the first 18 months of the Korean war was out of the question at the time of writing. Many commendations, it is true, attested to the high opinion of specific operations held by ground commanders. But such commendations, like the congratulatory statements by ground commanders about the ineffectual bombing of Cassino, could be premature or based on incomplete information, or might even be nothing more than expressions of service courtesy. The letters of commendation addressed to FEAF Bomber Command ranged from generalities about a task well done, as in General MacArthur's letters to the commanding officers of the 22d and 92d

Bombardment Groups at the time of the release of these groups to the Zone of Interior, to conscientious efforts to assess the damage wrought by medium bomber attacks in a specific action. A good example of a commendation of the latter type was a message sent on 21 May 1951 to the FEAF commanding general. On the day before, stated the message, a bombing attack hit the enemy only 400 yards ahead of the front lines of a U.N. infantry division near Sinchon. Twenty B-29's were dispatched of which 19 were vectored over troop concentrations by the controller. An American prisoner of war who managed to escape during the raid was quoted as saying that the greater part of a Chinese infantry battalion had been wiped out be the bombing, and that the resulting panic and disorganization prevented the enemy from carrying out their contemplated attack--all this despite the fact that the mission report indicated that the bombs fell 300 yards off the designated target. Other close support AN-MPQ-2 missions flown at night during this period accounted for a considerable number of enemy casualties.[34]

More convincing and informed opinions were expressed in the testimony taken down by Maj. Gen. Glenn O. Barcus's Air Power Evaluation Group in November 1950. The board concluded that B-29 maintenance in the Korean theater was at least as good as that in the United States, despite the fact that two groups flew to the combat zone on very short notice bringing with them only their 30-day flyaway kits. Further, the combat-sortie rate was considerably higher than could have been maintained during World War II, and the losses from all causes were only slightly higher than would be expected had the aircraft been engaged in operational training in the Zone of Interior. The compilers of the report were at pains to emphasize that the B-29 had fully demonstrated that it could be used in tactical situations under the special combat conditions prevailing in Korea. Its flexibility was far greater than had hitherto been supposed.[35]

One officer interviewed by the Barcus Board referred to the fact that the B-29 crews had all been trained to bomb from altitudes of 25,000 feet and above, with heavy stress on radar aids. In Korea, however, the bombardiers were releasing from altitudes as low as 4,000 feet. Moreover, they had successfully attacked pinpoint targets like bridges with the assistance of radar.[36] This accomplishment was most noteworthy in view of the poor record on bridge-busting missions made by the heavy bombers of World War II both in northern Italy and in Burma. A group intelligence officer, Capt. Norman Shaw, observed that the bomb line, which was posted daily in accordance with the ground situation, was studied carefully by bombardiers, and that not once had bombs been released below the bomb line to the peril of United Nations troops.[37] A third officer, a radar operator and bombardier of the 345th Bombardment Squadron, commented that because the currently used radar equipment operated best from altitudes of 18,000 to 30,000 feet, the radar bomb runs made at low altitude were not so effective as they might have been. He further stated, however, that on approximately 95 per cent of his missions bombs were dropped visually.[38]

Perhaps the best appraisal of the B-29's as tactical aircraft in Korea was to be found in the testimony of Maj. Gen. Emmett O'Donnell, Jr.

before the Congressional committees on Armed Services and Foreign Relations in June 1951. General O'Donnell testified that during the first three months of the war nearly two-thirds of the total medium bomber effort had been devoted to direct support, a conservative estimate in view of the figures cited earlier in this chapter.* He was careful to make clear that such assignment of strategic aircraft with their highly trained crews to tactical objectives could be justified only by special circumstances. Such special circumstances did, in his opinion, exist in Korea. The serious plight of the ground troops and the fact that insufficient numbers of light bombers and other tactical planes were available to the Fifth Air Force for the support of those forces were, of course, the principal justification for such use of the B-29. Moreover, the enemy's lack of an effective interceptor force and of antiaircraft artillery, especially during the first months of the war, made the tactical use of the B-29's less hazardous than it would otherwise have been. In response to questions by Senator Richard B. Russell, General O'Donnell stated that he regarded the employment of B-29's in close support, particularly in the bombing of supposed concentrations of enemy troops, as improper. He noted that the so-called saturation bombing at Waegwan was never proved to have accomplished anything and that it was doubtful that any sizeable concentration of enemy troops was there to be bombed. The supporting role for which he believed the B-29 had proved itself best suited in Korea was what he called "general support"—or the bombing of bridges and the interdiction of supply lines "a bit behind" the front lines.[39]

---

*See p. 134 above.

There can be no doubt that the B-29 made an important contribution to the Korean war even when functioning in a tactical capacity. Its efficiency in such a role, as compared with the heavy bombers in World War II, was in part due to improved radar bombing techniques.* But it must be remembered that against an enemy more liberally supplied with modern fighters and antiaircraft artillery the B-29's could scarcely be so employed. All tactical operations would then have to be taken over by faster, more maneuverable planes especially designed for such tasks.

---

*And after November 1951 its effectiveness was further increased by the substitution of shoran (AN-APN-3) radar equipment for the older AN-MPQ-2 equipment in all B-29's. Instead of the previous mere airborne search radar, shoran was a precision instrument consisting of two ground stations and an airborne transmitter and receiver with computer. The ground stations, when triggered by impulses from the airplane transmitter, signaled their positions on the airborne radarscope, and from these indications the location of the designated target could be very accurately determined. This system permitted blind bombing to be carried out from medium altitudes with an error no greater than 12.5 miles even when the ground stations were as distant as 140 miles from the target. In addition, shoran was useful in photomapping.

Chapter VII
CONCLUSION

Official recognition of the independence of strategic bombing was not forthcoming until as late as 1943.* In accordance with the concept of flexibility, realistic arrangements were at that time worked out for the diversion of strategic aircraft to tactical operations, when conditions warranted such a transfer. The objectives of strategic air power were defined as the sources of the enemy's war potential--that is, important industries, power plants, oil complexes, and communications centers. The primary responsibilities of tactical air power were to gain air superiority, isolate the battlefield, and provide close support to ground troops. Only when the ground forces found themselves in a dangerous situation, or when there was an especially good opportunity to punish a fleeing enemy should the strategic bombers be called away from their distant targets to add their weight to tactical operations. In the important respect that it protected the mission of strategic bombing from inordinate tactical demands, there can be no doubt about the soundness of this doctrine. The great strategic air assault on German-held Europe, according to the United States Strategic Bombing Survey, went very far toward winning the war in that theater before the first Allied soldier set foot on the beaches of Normandy.

---

* See p. 28.

AHS-88, Chap. VII

The primary purpose of the present study was to determine how closely the employment of strategic bombers in World War II and the first 18 months of the Korean war conformed to this doctrine. No attempt was made to describe with full statistical data all the nonstrategic missions flown by heavy and very heavy bombers in all theaters of World War II and in Korea. Rather, the review of combat experience in the Mediterranean theater, Europe, the Pacific, Asia, and Korea was for obvious reasons confined to accounts of only the most important close-support actions and of representative interdiction and counter-air operations. The reasons for the employment of strategic bombers in these roles were emphasized, and, whenever available, responsible evaluations of the tactical work of heavy bombers were cited.

The strategic targets available to the heavy bombers in the Mediterranean theater consisted mainly of ports and railroad yards until the Fifteenth Air Force began to range out from its Italian bases against CBO targets in Germany. To no small extent the B-17's and B-24's both in north Africa and in Italy were committed to antishipping work, interdiction programs such as STRANGLE, preinvasion strikes, and to battle-area or close-support bombing. The Eighth Air Force, on the other hand, was consistently reserved for strategic activities except when there was urgent need for supplementing the weight of the tactical air force, as in CROSSBOW and the landings in Normandy. After D-Day the strategic campaign was interrupted only occasionally by demands for close support and battlefield interdiction. In the Pacific areas, strategic targets were virtually nonexistent except in the home islands of Japan. Nevertheless, the heavy bomber, especially the B-24, proved indispensable for sea-search and counter-air operations because it was the only plane with sufficient range for such missions. Nearly all the strategic bombing in the war against Japan was performed by the B-29's, yet even the Twentieth Air Force was obliged to divert B-29's from their normal targets to hit troublesome air bases on Iwo Jima and later the kamikaze fields on Kyushu. In the Korean conflict to the end of 1951, on the other hand, the B-29's were heavily employed in a tactical capacity. Especially after the completion of the main strategic program in the autumn of 1950, the B-29's were steadily engaged in interdiction and even close-support tasks.

The above comparison of strategic bomber activities in the various theaters of World War II suggests immediately that the employment doctrine first formulated in Field Manual 100-20 of 1943 and which was implicit in later directives envisaged a theater of operations wherein significant strategic targets lay within range of the bombers. Clearly such conditions in World War II prevailed only in Europe. It is not too much to say that only the air forces based in England and on the continent were able to function in close conformity to the doctrine of Field Manual 100-20. Such campaigns as the long-range interdiction program conducted by the Fifteenth Air Force in northern Italy had evidently not been foreseen by the framers of this doctrine, nor did they seem to have had in mind the special conditions encountered in the air war in the Pacific. There, the need for a long-range striking force was paramount. B-17's and B-24's were consistently used against such elusive targets as ships at sea and in expensive forays against enemy air bases simply because they were the only planes which could reach these targets. Considerations of range aside, the proper weapons for such targets were the mediums and, sometimes, fighter-bombers, and the same could be said about the long-range interdiction objectives of the Fifteenth Air Force in Italy and some of the Tenth Air Force operations in Burma. The air forces in the Pacific and in most of the other theaters could have respected the distinction written into standard doctrine between tactical and strategic targets only if they could have been provided with medium and light bombers possessing the great range of the B-24.

A number of close-support missions of World War II were rather fully described in the preceding chapters. A clear evaluation of all of these actions, as has been shown, is difficult in the face of the occasionally contradictory testimony. One may state, however, that at Salerno, Anzio, Bologna, Saint-Lô, and Cape Gloucester, the heavies carried out their assigned tasks accurately, and their efforts were of benefit to the ground forces. At Cassino and in the preinvasion bombing of Normandy and southern France, the results were more questionable. The interdiction work of the heavies was also an indispensable piece in the pattern of victory, in spite of the difficulties experienced in hitting small targets like bridges and ships. The innumerable counter-air attacks, especially by the air forces in the Pacific, constituted another tactical mission performed with distinction by strategic bombers. Although all these close-support, interdiction, and counter-air tasks might have been more effectively and economically carried out by a similar weight of tactical bombers, the fact is that in most instances the strategic planes were the only air weapons at hand which could be sent over the target. On the whole, the skill of the crews in adapting strategic bombers to unfamiliar tactical missions is among the noteworthy features of the war. Yet it is certainly legitimate to suggest that the difficulties would have been materially lessened had the training of the aircrews been broadened to include such operations.

In Korea the early and continued use of B-29's in battlefield interdiction and even in close support was made possible only by a special set of circumstances. The enemy was not well provided with fighter planes until the conflict was well along, and by changes in tactics the loss of B-29's to enemy interception was kept well within tolerable limits even after the appearance of the MIG-15's in battle. Efficient antiaircraft artillery was also acquired by the enemy at a rather late date. The discovery that the B-29's could work effectively at night with radar aids and even make hits on pinpoint targets such as bridges tended to justify their continuance in a tactical role.

Two factors appear to be crucial in the success of virtually all close- and general support missions flown by strategic aircraft: control and damage assessment. By control is meant the marking of the bomb line, preferably by radar or electronic beacons; the establishment of a radio net by means of which ground forces reports of target locations or of bombing errors can be promptly communicated to the bomber formations; and finally, target identification.

The heavy bomber efforts at Metz-Thionville and Eschweiler illustrated especially well the value of such controls. At Eschweiler, Army sources reported the single accidental bomb release so promptly that all other bombers could be ordered to close their bomb-bay doors before they crossed their own lines. On the other hand, the relatively minor battlefield attacks flown against the Japanese defenders on Attu in May 1943 served to indicate the dangers arising from inadequate controls. Again, the partial failure of the massive bomber attacks at Caen and Saint-Lô in July and August 1944 were due directly to inadequate target identification. And the equally ineffectual marking of the bomb line was responsible for the many deaths resulting from the short bombing on both these missions.

The second factor, one which seems repeatedly to have plagued the mission planners, was the great need for, and the almost inevitable difficulty of, assessing the damage inflicted on the enemy by support bombing, whether by strategic or tactical aircraft. In the preinvasion bombings of World War II, the problem of ascertaining to what extent enemy installations were knocked out by aerial attack, sometimes supplemnted by naval bombardment, was a crucial one. But it also assumed importance in carpet bombing attacks, such as those at Saint-Lô in France and Waegwan in Korea, laid on to lend support to land operations.

The preinvasion attacks on the Normandy beaches on 6 June 1944 and on the beaches of southern France two months later were not unqualified successes. The heavy bomber assault on Normandy left many shore-line defenses untouched, and in southern France even the best concentrations of bomb bursts often failed to damage gun emplacements. Still, both attacks were sufficiently powerful to stun the enemy defenders and to reduce their morale and efficiency substantially. The attack on Tarawa, or Betio, in November 1944, which was delivered by some 50 B-24 sorties and also by a heavy naval barrage, neither destroyed enemy installations nor daunted the defenders to any marked degree.

Two general conclusions may be drawn from this study. One, doctrine must be modified with reference to combat conditions in a given theater if it is to serve as an effective guide to the conduct of air warfare in that theater. Perhaps the most important of these conditions is whether the theater contains sufficient industrial and other objectives to justify a systematic strategic campaign. Such geographic considerations as the range required of medium bombers and attack planes for interdicting the enemy's supplies and reinforcements must also be weighed. Two, the occasional need in modern warfare to divert strategic bombers to certain tactical roles should receive explicit recognition in the operational training given the aircrews. The present review of combat experience further suggests that most of those tactical missions which must be classified as not fully successful were characterized either by failure to provide proper controls in the form of adequate target information and bomb-line markers or by a tendency on the part of the planners to expect much more of the heavy bombers in support actions than they were capable of delivering, especially in carpet bombing or invasion beach attacks.

FOOTNOTES

Chapter I

1. H. A. Jones, *The War in the Air, Being the Story of the Part Played in the Great War by the Royal Air Force* (Oxford, 1922-1937), IV, 260 ff.; J. A. Chamier, *The Birth of the Royal Air Force* (London, 1943), pp. 171-74.

2. WD Hist. Div., Anzio Beachhead (1944), p. 77, in 171.1-6; Hist. 12th AF, V (the Central Italian Campaign), 33-35. Unless otherwise indicated, all documents are located in the Archives of the USAF Historical Division, Maxwell AFB, Ala.

3. AHS-71, United States Air Force Operations in the Korean Conflict 25 June-1 November 1950, p. 35; FEAF Opns. Hist., 25 June-31 Oct. 1950, I, 53, in K-720.302A.

4. Hist. 19th Bomb. Gp., 26 June-31 Oct. 1950, p. 11.

5. Testimony of Maj. Gen. Emmett O'Donnell, Jr., *Hearings Before the Committee on Armed Services and the Committee on Foreign Relations*, U. S. Senate, 82 Cong. 1 Sess., 3,065.

6. Combat histories of several of the air forces in World War II speak of the impossibility of classifying certain operations as strategic or tactical. See The History of the Fifteenth Air Force, Nov.-1944-May 1945, I, 289-99, for a discussion of the difficulty of classifying attacks on enemy communications.

7. These two types of tactical missions are defined in Joint Training Directive for Air-Ground Operations, 1 Sept. 1950, p. 9, in K-417.549A, a document which is analyzed in Chapter II.

8. AHS-30, Ninth Air Force in the Western Desert Campaign to 23 January 1943, p. 24.

9. AFR 55-23, 23 July 1953, designated the B-36 and B-52 as heavy bombers; the B-29, B-50 (a modification of the B-29) and the B-47 as medium bombers; and the B-26, B-45, B-57, and B-66 as light bombers. Procurement of the B-36 has been halted in favor of the jet-powered B-52, which will eventually supplant it as the first-line strategic bomber.

10. The Air Force in Theaters of Operations: Organization and Functions, May 1943, Bklt. I, p. 2 ff., in 168.11-4.

11. AHS-32, Ninth Air Force in the ETO, 16 October 1943-16 April 1944, p. 145.

AHS-30, Notes, Chap. I

12. The disadvantages inherent in the use of heavy bombers against tactical objectives are discussed in Army Air Forces Evaluation Board, Mediterranean Theater of Operations, Vol. I, Pt. II, p. 9, in 138.5-1, and Pt. V, pp. 2 ff., in 138.5-2. See also in this same connection 8th AF, Close-In Air Cooperation by Heavy Bombers with Ground Forces, p. 5 ff., in 520.4501A; and Air Staff and Command School, The Feasibility of Low and Minimum Altitude Bombing by Strategic Bombers, in AU Lib. M-32984-S, C297f.

13. AHS-70, Tactical Operations of the Eighth Air Force, 6 June 1944 to 8 May 1945, p. 62 ff.

14. AAF Eval. Bd., MTO, Vol. I, Pt. V, p. 63, in 138.5-2.

15. Omar N. Bradley, A Soldier's Story (New York, 1951), pp. 346-49.

16. Sir Arthur Harris, Bomber Offensive (New York, 1947), pp. 56, 210.

AHS-88

FOOTNOTES

Chapter II

1. H. A. Jones, *The War in the Air, Being the Story of the Part Played in the Great War by the Royal Air Force* (Oxford, 1922-1937), IV, 453; *The Times History of the War* (London, 1919), XIX, 284 ff.; Air Corps Tactical School, Bombardment Aviation, Feb. 1931, p. 8, in 248.101-9.

2. The United States Strategic Bombing Survey: Over-all Report (European War) (Washington, 30 Sept. 1945), p. 107, in 137.301-1.

3. Field Service Regs., USA, 1923, p. 23.

4. Ibid., p. 21.

5. TR 440-15, 26 Jan. 1926, p. 1.

6. Ibid., pp. 11-12.

7. An excellent discussion of the struggle for proper recognition of the air arm during this period of the slow growth of the concept of strategic bombing is to be found in *The Army Air Forces in World War II*, ed. W. F. Craven and J. L. Cate, I (Chicago, 1948), Chap. 2.

8. Air Service Tac. Sch., Bombardment, 1924-1925, pp. 2-7, in 248.101-9.

9. ACTS, The Air Force, Feb. 1931, pp. 12, 37-39, in 248.1011-189.

10. Ibid., p. 16.

11. ACTS, Bombardment Aviation, pp. 68-69.

12. Ibid., p. 136.

13. The Air Corps purchased 63 bombardment aircraft, all of them Keystone B-3A's, during the fiscal year 1930. See Aeronautical Chamber of Commerce of America, Inc., *The Aircraft Yearbook for 1931* (New York, 1931), p. 545.

14. AHS-6, The Development of the Heavy Bomber, 1918-1944, pp. 63 ff.

15. TR 440-15, 15 Oct. 1935, p. 3.

16. Ibid., p. 5.

17. Ibid., p. 5-6.

AHS-33, Notes, Chap. II   159

18. Ibid., p. 5.

19. AAF in World War II, I, 48-49.

20. ACTS, The Air Force, p. 38.

21. See the discussion of the Joint Army-Navy Board paper of September 1934 on the employment of the GHQ Air Force, in AAF in World War II, I, 48.

22. FM 1-5, 1940, p. 29.

23. Ibid.

24. Tng. Cir. 52, 29 Aug. 1941, pp. 5-6.

25. Ibid., pp. 5-6.

26. Ibid., p. 6.

27. Ibid.,

28. Tng. Cir. 70, 16 Dec. 1941, p. 7.

29. Ibid., p. 9.

30. FM 31-35, 9 Apr. 1942, pp. 10 ff.

31. Ibid., p. 17.

32. See the discussion in draft AHS, The Development of Air Doctrine in the U. S. Air Force, 1917-1951, p. 19.

33. Ibid., pp. 20 ff. A description of some specific actions in the desert campaign will be found in Chapter III of the present study. See also AAF School of Applied Tactics, Mission of Tactical Bombardment, Part II, Tactical Bombardment in the North African and Mediterranean Theaters, Jan. 1944.

34. See AAF in World War II, II, 163-65, and also draft AHS, Development of Air Doctrine, p. 20 ff.

35. Ltr., Col. Charles G. Williamson, C/Status of Opns. Div., D/Bomb. to D/Bomb., Hq. AAF, 3 Mar. 1943.

36. The Air Force in Theaters of Operations: Organization and Functions, Pamphlet No. 4, p. 34, in 168.11-4.

37. FM 100-20, 21 July 1943, p. 1, in 170.12-6.

38. Ibid., p. 3.

AHS-80, Notes, Chap. II

39. Ibid., pp. 4-9.

40. Ibid., pp. 10-12.

41. Ibid., p. 9.

42. Ibid., p. 10.

43. FM 31-35, Aug. 1946.

44. Proposed revision of FM 31-35 by John W. Hansborough, Lt. Col., Field Artillery, Mar. 1949.

45. Some Notes on the Use of Air Power in Support of Land Operations and Direct Air Support (Holland, Dec. 1944), in Air Support for Ground Forces (SCS) RG 910, in AG 373.21.

46. OC/AFF and Hq. TAC, Joint Training Directive for Air-Ground Operations, 1 Sept. 1950, pp. 175-76.

47. Ibid., p. 175.

48. Ibid., pp. 175-79.

49. Ibid., pp. 185-86.

50. Ibid., pp. 8-9.

51. The transition training in effect during 1939 for the B-17 did not include any close-support tactics, although some hours of training were devoted to low-altitude bombing. See AHS-18, Pilot Transition to Combat Aircraft, pp. 23-25, and app. 1. Further, there is no indication that the OTU-RTU program during World War II included such close-support training (AHS-18, pp. 68-75 ff.).

52. TR 440-15, 26 Jan. 1926, p. 11.

53. TR 440-15, 15 Oct. 1935, p. 5.

54. Tng. Cir. 70, 16 Dec. 1941, p. 5.

55. FM 100-20, 21 July 1943, p. 9.

56. 8th AF, Close-In Air Cooperation by Heavy Bombers with Ground Forces, p. 3, in 520-4501A.

57. USSES, Over-all Report (European War), pp. 63-64.

58. Ibid., p. 51.

AHS-88, Notes, Chap. II 161

59. ACTS, The Air Force, p. 39.
60. Hansborough proposed revision.
61. Hist. 15th AF, Nov. 1944-May 1945, I, 298-99.

NOTES

Chapter III

1. Army Air Forces Evaluation Board, Mediterranean Theater of Operations, Vol. I, Evaluation of Tactical and Strategic Operations, Pt. III, p. 17 ff., in 138.5 /hereinafter cited as AAF Eval. Bd., MTO/.

2. AAF in World War II, II, 3 ff.; AHS-30, Ninth Air Force in the Western Desert Campaign, p. 2 ff.

3. AAF in World War II, II, 12 ff.; and AHS-30, p. 77 ff.

4. See fuller account in AAF in World War II, II, 108.

5. AAF in World War II, II, 161 ff.; AHS-14, the Twelfth Air Force in the North African Winter Campaign, p. 1 ff.; Hist. XII BC, 20 Aug. 1942-1 Jan. 1943.

6. RAF Middle East Review, No. 1, pp. 35-36 in 512.609C. The information in this source is fully utilized in AAF in World War II, II, 36 ff.

7. AHS-30, p. 70 ff.; AAF in World War II, II, 36 ff.

8. AAF in World War II, II, 145 ff.

9. RAF Middle East Review, No. 2, p. 34. Capt. Rowan T. Thomas, pilot of a B-17, "Judge's Jury," records, however, that the heavies bombed German troops in the pass itself (Thomas, Born in Battle /Philadelphia, 1944/, p. 339).

10. In addition to the discussion of the air phase of the Kasserine battle in AAF in World War II, II, 153 ff., one can get interesting sidelights from Heinz Werner Schmidt, With Rommel in the Desert (London, 1951), p. 196 ff.

11. AAF Eval. Bd., MTO, Vol. I, Pt. III, p. 17.

12. Ltr., Col. Charles G. Williamson, C/Status of Opns. Div. D/B to D/Bomb., Hq., AAF, 3 Mar. 1943.

13. AAF in World War II, II, 108.

14. Ibid., II, 124-25.

15. Ibid., II, 419 ff., and 432-34.

AHS-88, Notes, Chap. III

16. *Ibid.*, II, 434-45.

17. *Ibid.*, II, 460-77; RAF Middle East Review, No. 4.

18. *AAF in World War II*, II, 488-93; AHS-15, Air Phase of the Italian Campaign to 1 January 1944, pp. 49 ff.

19. MATAF Operational Rpts., p. 12, in 626.310.

20. AHS-15, p. 108 ff.; *AAF in World War II*, II, 520-29.

21. MATAF Operational Rpts., p. 20.

22. See British Air Ministry translation VII/98, The Campaign in Italy, chap. VII, /General Westphal/, The Army Group's Version, p. 8, in 512.621, v. 32. Such studies speak with respect of the unified command arrangements under which the Allies were able to call up heavy air attacks at Salerno and elsewhere in Italy, but little attention is given to discriminating between the effects of bombardment of heavy and of tactical aircraft.

23. AAF Eval. Bd., MTO, Vol. I, Pt. V, pp. 17-18.

24. RAF Mediterranean Review, No. 5, p. 28.

25. *AAF in World War II*, II, 564 ff.

26. Hist. 15th AF, Nov. 1943-May 1945, I, 408-10; *AAF in World War II*, III, 358-59.

27. Operation BIGOT-SHINGLE, in Mediterranean Allied Air Forces Operations in Support of SHINGLE, 1 Jan.-15 Feb. 1944, in 168.61-1.

28. *AAF in World War II*, III, 340-43.

29. *Ibid.*, III, 339 ff.

30. DA Hist. Div., Anzio Beachhead (1944), p. 77 ff.; Hist. 15th AF, Nov. 1943-May 1945, I, 450-54.

31. See British Air Ministry translation VII/100, The Campaign in Italy: Special Subjects, chap. I, /Col. Ernst Faehndrich/ The Supply Situation, pp. 11-12, in 512.621 v. 34.

32. Anzio Beachhead, p. 77 ff.; Hist. 15th AF, Nov. 1943-May 1945, I, 450-54.

33. *AAF in World War II*, III, 359-60.

AHS-83, Notes, Chap. III   164

34. See General Dever's statement quoted in AAF in World War II, III, 357.

35. The figures cited here, as with most of the other actions described in this chapter, are taken from the Army Air Forces Evaluation Board Report. Some differences which the available data do not permit one to reconcile are to be found in the statistics cited in the History of the Fifteenth Air Force, November 1943-May 1945, Vol. I.

36. AAF Eval. Bd., MTO, Vol. I, Pt. III, p. 2.

37. Ibid., p. 20.

38. AAF in World War II, III, 356.

39. See AAF in World War II, III, 361-70 for a discussion of the controversy over the bombings of Cassino.

40. AAF Eval. Bd., MTO, Vol. I, Pt. III, pp. 24, 72-73. The History of the Fifteenth Air Force, November 1943-May 1945, Vol. I, 454, speaks of 142 B-17's dropping 353 tons of bombs.

41. Hist. 15th AF, Nov. 1943-May 1945, I, 454-55.

42. AAF in World War II, III, 363-66.

43. AAF Eval. Bd., MTO, Vol. I, Pt. III, pp. 22, 72-73.

44. AAF in World War II, III, 368-69; British Air Ministry translation VII/97, The Campaign in Italy, chap. VI [Gen. von Vietinghoff] A Post-War Study, pp. 59-60, in 512.621v.31.

45. AAF in World War II, III, 367.

46. Allied Force Hq., Tng. Memo No. 5, 4 June 1944, Lessons from the Cassino Operation, 15-25 Mar. 1944, in Air Support for Ground Forces, (SGS) RG 910, in AG 373.21.

47. Ibid., III, 373-83. See also British Air Ministry translation VII/100, The Supply Situation, p. 14.

48. AAF Eval. Bd., MTO, Vol. I, Pt. III, pp. 24-27, 72-73. The History of the Fifteenth Air Force, November 1943-May 1945, I, 457 states that 689 bombers dropped 1,762 tons of bombs.

49. AAF Eval. Bd., MTO, Vol. I, Pt. III, p. 74.

50. Another mission which must be considered tactical was a raid by heavies on 12 May, the day DIADEM got under way, of Marshal Kesselring's headquarters and also the headquarters of the German X Corps. Both objectives were well hit (Hist. 15th AF, Nov. 1943-May 1945, I, 457).

AHS-38, Notes, Chap. III 165

51. AAF Eval. Bd., MTO, Vol. I, Pt. III, pp. 28-34; MATAF Opnl. Rpts.; AAF in World War II, III, 425-27; Hq. AAF, Wings at War Series, No. 1, The AAF in the Invasion of Southern France (Washington, 1945).

52. AAF Eval. Bd., MTO, Vol. I, Pt. III, pp. 34-38. See Also AAF in World War II, III, 428, for a favorable assessment of the results of YOKUM.

53. AAF Eval. Bd., MTO, Vol. I, Pt. III, pp. 38-42.

54. AAF in World War II, III, 472-73.

55. Hist. 15th AF, Nov. 1943-May 1945, I, 457 ff.; AAF Eval. Bd., MTO, Vol. I, Pt. III, p. 12 ff.

56. AAF Eval. Bd., MTO, Vol. I, Pt. III, pp. 42-63.

57. Hist. 15th AF, Nov. 1943-May 1945, I, 458 ff.; AAF in World War II, III, 483-89.

58. AC/AS Intel. Hist. Div., Review of Aerial Warfare for the Scientific Advisory Board, Jan. 1945, pp. 30-34, in 105-5.

AHS-88, Notes, Chap. IV   167

16. As a result of this event, Eisenhower is said to have considered ordering all heavy bombers operating in close support to fly parallel rather than perpendicular to friendly lines (H. C. Butcher, *My Three Years with Eisenhower* (New York, 1946), pp. 636, 641).

17. 8th AF Rpt., pp. 34-35; AAF in World War II, III, 250-51.

18. 8th AF Rpt., pp. 3, 34-35.

19. *Ibid.*, pp. 28-30; AHS-70, pp. 53-54.

20. 8th AF Rpt., pp. 28-30; *AAF in World War II*, III, 229-30; AHS-70, p. 54.

21. AAF in World War II, III, 230.

22. 8th AF Rpt., pp. 49-51; *AAF in World War II*, III, 233-34; AHS-70, pp. 55-56.

23. 8th AF Rpt., p. 32. A short review of prisoner-of-war interrogations pertaining to this action and of official appraisals made by the XIX Corps and other U.S. Army organizations appears in *AAF in World War II*, III, 234-37. General Eisenhower and Marshal von Rundstedt are both quoted here to the effect that the battle of Saint-Lô was won as a direct result of the Eighth Air Force bombing.

24. *AAF in World War II*, III, 237-38.

25. 8th AF Rpt., p. 40; *AAF in World War II*, III, 624.

26. 8th AF Rpt., pp. 40-41.

27. *Ibid.*, pp. 41-44; AHS-70, p. 67 ff.

28. 8th AF Rpt., pp. 44-45; and AHS-70, pp. 69-70.

29. 1st U.S. Army, Rpt. of Opns., 1 Aug. 1944-22 Feb. 1945, pp. 67-73.

30. FO 1314, in 1st Air Div., The Eschweiler Mission, 16 Nov. 1944, in 525.04A.

31. AHS-70, p. 71.

32. 8th AF TMR, Opn. No. 715, 16 Nov. 1944, in 520.331.

33. *Ibid.*

34. *Ibid.*

AHS-88

NOTES

Chapter IV

1. *AAF in World War II*, III, 131, 280.

2. *Ibid.*, III, 140 ff.

3. *Ibid.*, III, 279, 319, 321-22; 8th AF, The Tactical Use of Heavy Bombardment in the Normandy Invasion, in 520.04 L; and AHS-70, Tactical Operations of the Eighth Air Force, 6 June 1944 to 8 May 1945, p. 3 ff.

4. From 8th AF. Close-in Air Cooperation by Heavy Bombers with Ground Forces, pp. 2-3, in 520.4501A /hereafter referred to as 8th AF Rpt./.

5. *AAF in World War II*, III, 138 ff.; WD Hist. Div., Utah Beach to Cherbourg, 6-27 June 1944 in 171.1-12; WD Hist Div., Omaha Beachhead, 6-13 June 1944; Hq. AAF, Wings at War Series, No. 2, *Sunday Punch in Normandy* (Washington, 1945).

6. 8th AF Rpt., pp. 31-32.

7. *Ibid.*, p. 36 ff.; *AAF in World War II*, III, 190 ff.; AHS-70, p. 24 ff.

8. 8th AF Rpt., pp. 37-38; AHS-70, p. 24 ff.; 8th AF, Use of Heavies in Normandy.

9. 8th AF Rpt., pp. 37-38; 8th AF, Use of Heavies in Normandy.

10. 8th AF Rpt., p. 38.

11. *Ibid.*, pp. 38-39.

12. Questionnaires submitted by the Air Effects Committee, 12th Army Group, cited in *AAF in World War II*, III, 192-93.

13. 8th AF Rpt., p. 3.

14. *AAF in World War II*, III, 207-8.

15. 8th AF Rpt., pp. 33-34; AHS-70, p. 57 ff.; *AAF in World War II*, III, 207-9.

AHS-88, Notes, Chap. IV

35. 8th AF Rpt., pp. 36-37; AAF in World War II, III, 631-32; AHS-70, pp. 70-72.

36. 8th AF Rpt., pp. 81-83; AHS-70, pp. 72-73.

37. 8th AF Rpt., pp. 83-84.

38. 1st Army special report, Effects of Our Air Attacks of 16 November, a Study; see also memo for C/S from AC/AS SHAEF, sub.: Effects of Close Support Operations by Heavy Bombers, 30 Nov. 1944, in Air Support for Ground Forces (SGS) RG 910, in AG 373.21.

39. 1st Air Div., Eschweiler Mission.

40. AAF in World War II, III, 672-85.

41. Ibid., III, 685-86; AHS-70, pp. 74-77.

42. 8th AF Rpt., pp. 133-40; AHS-70, p. 78 ff.

43. AAF in World War II, III, 693-711; AHS-70, p. 79 ff.

44. AC/AS Intel. Hist. Div., Review of Aerial Warfare for the Scientific Advisory Board, Jan. 1945, pp. 37-41, in 105.5

45. SHAEF, Use of Heavy Bombers in a Tactical Role, in Air Support for Ground Forces (SGS) RG 910, in AG 373.21.

AHS-83

FOOTNOTES

Chapter V

1. AAF in World War II, IV, 90.

2. Ibid., IV, 231.

3. Samuel E. Morison, History of the United States Naval Operations in World War II (Boston, 1949), IV, 249-50.

4. Intelligence Summaries /hereinafter referred to as Isum/ #17, 36th Bomb. Sq. (H), 23 May 1943; #51, XI BC, 24 May 1943; #18, 36th Bomb. Sq. (H), 24 May 1943; #52, XI BC, 26 May 1943. See also AAF in World War II, IV, 385-86.

5. Aleutian Campaign, Navy, Dec. 1941-Dec. 1944. See also FO 10, Hq. 11th AF, 25 Apr. 1943, in Hist. 11th AF (A-3), Ref. No. 24.

6. Interview with Brig. Gen. William E. Lynd; Isum #52, XI BC, 25 May 1943.

7. Interview with Gen. Lynd.

8. See especially Isum #53, XI BC, 26 May 1943.

9. Diary of Neru Tatuskuchi, Actg. Off., Northern 5316 Det. (1943).

10. For a soldier's view of the short bombing, see WD, The Capture of Attu as Told by the Men Who Fought There (Washington, 1944), pp. 82-83. See also AAF in World War II, IV, 385.

11. Isum #52, XI BC, 25 May 1943.

12. AAF in World War II, IV, 359-401.

13. AHS-38, Operations History of the Seventh Air Force, 6 November 1943 to 31 July 1944, chronology of 7th AF operations in appendix. See also AAF in World War II, IV, 201, 298, 672-93; USSES, Air Campaigns of the Pacific War (Washington, 1947), in 137.715-71A /hereinafter cited USSBS, Air Campaigns/.

14. AHS-38, p. 8 ff.

15. Seventh Air Force Participation in the GALVANIC Operation, 13 Nov-6 Dec. 1943; ltr., Maj. Gen. Willis H. Hale, sub.: Operations of the Seventh Air Force, 13 Nov. 1943-31 Jan. 1944, 15 Feb. 1944; AHS-38, pp. 8-9; Advon Hq. 7th AF, Report of Strike Operations During the GALVANIC Action, in 740.3069-10.

AHS-38, Notes, Chap. V   170

16. AAF Eval. Bd., POA, Rpt. #1, p. 55, in 138.6-1. See also AHS-38, p. 12.

17. USSBS, Air Campaigns, p. 28.

18. AAF Eval. Bd., POA, Rpt. #1, p. 12. See also AHS-38, p. 12.

19. Ltr., Lt. Gen. Robert C. Richardson, Jr., Hq. USA Forces CENPAC to CinC POA, 6 Dec. 1943.

20. Capt. James R. Stockman, Hist. Sec., USMC, The Battle for Tarawa (1947), p. 67, in 186.1-1.

21. Hq. AAF, Wings at War Series, No. 3, Pacific Counterblow (Washington, 1945), p. 32.

22. Memo for King from Arnold, 17 Dec. 1942, in 750.31. See also AAF in World War II, IV, 61-74.

23. AAF in World War II, IV, 241-43.

24. WD Hist. Div., The Admiralties (Washington, 1944), pp. 18, 70, etc., in 171.1-8; Activation History of the XIII Bomber Command, 13 Jan. 1943-1 Jan. 1944; AAF in World War II, IV, 74-91, 646 ff.

25. USSBS, Air Campaigns, pp. 42 ff.; AC/AS Intel. Hist. Div., Review of Aerial Warfare for the Scientific Advisory Board, p. 72; AAF in World War II, V, 316-22.

26. Hist. XIII BC, Jan. 1945, pp. 2-3, 71.

27. USSBS, Air Campaigns, p. 51.

28. GHQ FEC Mil. Hist. Sec., Battle of the Bismarck Sea, in 712.04A; AAF in World War II, IV, 98 ff.

29. USSBS, Air Campaigns, pp. 18-19, 24-25, 41, 51.

30. AHS-13, The Fifth Air Force in the Huon Peninsula Campaign, January to October 1943, pp. 209, 220, 227. There is an appendix summarizing bombardment operations against various New Guinea targets. These are called "bombardment operations in support of ground operations," yet it is clear that the title is loosely applied since ground forces were not in close proximity to any of these targets.

31. AHS-16, The Fifth Air Force in the Huon Peninsula Campaign, October 1943 to September 1944, p. 161.

32. AHS-43, The Fifth Air Force in the Conquest of the Bismarck Archipelago, p. 37 ff. See also unit histories for close records of these operations--for example, Hist. 19th Bomb. Sq., Feb.-Mar. 1944 and Apr. 1944.

AHS-85, Notes, Chap. V

33. AHS-43, p. 118.

34. AAF in World War II, IV, 657-58.

35. AHS-43, p. 61.

36. Ibid., p. 66.

37. See, for example, ltr., Maj. Gen. J. M. Swing, CG 11th Airborne Div. to CO 8th Ftr. Gp., 4 May 1945.

38. USSBS, Air Campaigns, pp. 9-10, 12; AAF in World War II, IV, 429-33.

39. AAF in World War II, IV, 488-93.

40. Ibid., IV, 473-83.

41. Ibid., IV, 493-515.

42. USSBS, Air Campaigns, p. 46 ff.

43. Ibid., pp. 9-21; AAF in World War II, IV, 440-540.

44. USSBS, Air Campaigns, pp. 20-50.

45. Ibid., pp. 43-53; USSBS, Summary Report, Pacific War (Washington, 1946), p. 16 /hereinafter cited USSBS, Summary Report/, in 137.701-1.

46. USSBS, Air Campaigns, pp. 43-53; USSBS, Summary Report, p. 10 ff.

47. USSBS, Summary Report, pp. 16-22.

48. An important reason for the paucity of close support missions assigned to heavy bombers was that in ground battles taking place in the kind of jungle covering many of the Pacific islands there was no long and continuous front. Instead, ground troops often fought in isolated groups. To distinguish from the air any military targets in such a battle, let alone a bomb line separating friend from foe, was impossible. See draft AHS, Air Support in the Pacific War 1941-1945, p. 1.

49. AC/AS Intel., Hist. Div., Review of Aerial Warfare, p. 97.

50. Ibid., pp. 93 ff. In the final statistical summaries of the sinking of Japanese shipping, however, AAF operations show up very well. Out of an estimated total tonnage of 10,100,000, no less than 8,900,000 tons of Japanese merchant ships were sunk or badly damaged. Of this amount, 54.7 per cent was attributed to submarines, 16.3 per cent to carrier-based air, 10.2 per cent to AAF land-based planes, 4.3 per cent to Navy and Marine land-based planes, and 9.3 per cent to mines, largely dropped by B-29's. Of course, a good part of the tonnage credited to the AAF was sunk or damaged by tactical aircraft. See USSBS, Summary Report, p. 16.

51. AC/AS Intel., Review of Aerial Warfare, p. 87.
52. *Ibid.*, p. 66.

NOTES

Chapter VI

1. AHS-71, United States Air Force Operations in the Korean Conflict 25 June-1 November 1950, pp. 1-3 and 81 ff.; FEAF Opns. Hist., 25 June-31 Oct. 1950, I, 41-42, 47, 91, 348, 354 in K-720.302A; ltr., Hq. UN Comd. to CO 92d Bomb. Sq., 24 Oct. 1952.

2. FEAF Opns. Hist., 25 June-31 Oct. 1950, I, 24-38.

3. Hist. Hq. 19th Bomb. Gp., 26 June-31 Oct. 1950, p. 11.

4. FEAF Opns. Hist., 25 June-31 Oct. 1950, I, 40-43.

5. Ibid., pp. 42-56.

6. Maj. Gen. William F. Dean credited air power with this achievement. See Robert F. Futrell and Albert F. Simpson, "Air War in Korea: II," Air University Quarterly Review (Spring 1951), pp. 59-63.

7. AHS-71, pp. 9-13.

8. Hist. FEAF BC, 1 Feb.-30 June 1951, Vol. I, Bk. IV, p. 10.

9. Ibid., p. 13.

10. Col. Raymond S. Sleeper, "Korean Targets for Medium Bombardment," Air University Quarterly Review (Spring 1951), pp. 23-24.

11. FEAF Opns. Hist., 25 June-31 Oct. 1950, I, 56-238.

12. Futrell and Simpson, "Air War," p. 67.

13. AHS-71, pp. 81-89.

14. FEAF Opns. Hist., 25 June-31 Oct. 1950, I, 90-250; FEAF Wkly. Intel. Roundup, under appropriate dates, in K-720.607A.

15. FEAF Opns. Hist., 25 June-31 Oct. 1950, I, 110-13; AHS-71, p. 47.

16. Testimony of Maj. Gen. Emmett O'Donnell, Jr., Hearings Before the Committee on Armed Services and the Committee on Foreign Relations, U.S. Senate, 82 Cong. 1 Sess. Pt. 4, p. 3066.

17. FEAF Opns. Hist., 25 June-31 Oct. 1950, I, 115.

AHS-88, Notes, Chap. VI

18. FEAF Opns. Hist., 1 Nov. 1950-28 Feb. 1951, II, 159.

19. Ibid., p. 127.

20. Col. Willis G. Carter, "Strategic Bombardment and National Objectives," Air University Quarterly Review (Spring 1951), pp. 5-14.

21. FEAF Wkly. Intel. Roundup, under appropriate dates.

22. Ibid.

23. FEAF Opns. Hist., 1 Nov. 1950-28 Feb. 1951, II, 87.

24. Ibid., pp. 109-59.

25. Ibid., pp. 160-299; FEAF Wkly. Intel. Roundup, under appropriate dates.

26. FEAF Wkly. Intel. Roundups, under appropriate dates.

27. Hist. 19th Bomb. Wg., July 1951, app.

28. Hist. FEAF, 1 July-31 Dec. 1951, I, 54-57.

29. Ibid., I, 42-44, and 58.

30. Ibid., I, 58-98.

31. Ibid., I, 60; FEAF Wkly. Intel. Roundup, Dec. 1951.

32. FEAF BC, Final Mission Summaries, Feb.-June 1951, pp. 1-3.

33. Ibid., p. 4 ff.

34. Reproduced in Hist. FEAF BC, 4 July-4 Oct. 1950, Vol. I, Bk. IV, app. See this and other Eighth Army reports on bombing effectiveness in Hist. FEAF, 1 Jan.-30 June 1951, p. 54 ff. See also the reports of missions Nos. 419-21, 18-20 May 1951, in FEAF BC, Final Mission Summaries, Feb.-June 1951, Vol. II, Pt. 4, and Final Draft, Report from the Secretary of Defense to the President of the United States on Operations in Korea During the Period 25 June 1950-8 July 1951, Pt. VII, p. 16.

35. Maj. Gen. Glenn O. Barcus, et al., an Evaluation of the United States Air Force in the Korean Campaign, pp. 1 ff, in K168.1504A.

36. Ibid., pp. 55-67, testimony of Maj. James W. Miller, Group Standardization Board Bombardier.

37. Ibid., pp. 67-70.

AHS-88, Notes, Chap. VI

38. *Ibid.*, pp. 35-36, testimony of Major Turbak.

39. Hearings, U.S. Senate, 82 Cong., 1 Sess., Pt. 4, p. 3062 ff.

40. On 30 November 1951, 36 shoran installations were completed on B-29's and 78 additional equipments were installed during December (Hist. FEAF, 1 July-31 Dec. 1951, Bk. I, Vol. II, pp. 70-74).

INDEX

A

A-20, 45, 113
Aachen, 88
AAF Evaluation Board, 40, 65, 67-68, 106; Ordnance Division, 67
AAF School of Applied Tactics, 27
Adak, 101
Admiralty Is., 109
Adriatic Sea, 64
Africa, 4, 10, 24-27, 39-48, 71, 73, 150
Air Corps Act (2 July 1926), 14
Air Corps Tactical School, 14, 16, 33, 37
Air Force Combat Command, 22. See also GHQ Air Force
Air Forces (numbered):
  Second Tactical (RAF), 74, 79, 94
  Third Tactical (RAF), 116
  Fifth, 110-13, 121, 125, 127-29, 132, 136-37, 147
  Seventh, 104-6, 109-11, 121
  Eighth, 4-5, 36, 42, 55, 73-77, 80-83, 86, 89-96, 150
  Ninth, 5, 42-43, 49, 74, 79, 81, 89, 94
  Tenth, 41, 113-18, 121, 152
  Eleventh, 100-4, 119
  Twelfth, 25, 42-43, 48, 55
  Thirteenth, 108-11
  Fourteenth, 113, 115-18, 121
  Fifteenth, 1, 4, 37-38, 51, 55-57, 59, 61-62, 64, 66, 69-71, 74, 77, 150-52
  Twentieth, 111, 125, 127, 151
Air Power Evaluation Group, 145-46
Air Transport Command, 116
Alam Halfa, 43, 46
Alaska, 99
Albano Laziale, 58

Aldenhoven, 89
Aleutians, 99-104
Alexander, Gen. Harold L., 54
Algeria, 42-43
Allen, Maj. Gen. Terry, 94
Allied Air Force, 111
Allied Air Support Command, 45-46
Allied Expeditionary Air Forces, 74
Allied Force Headquarters, 63
Amchitka, 101
American Volunteer Group, 117
Ancona, 56
Andaman Sea, 117
Andong, 128
Antung, 136
ANVIL, 39, 66
Anzio, 1, 3, 51, 55-60, 65, 72, 80, 152
Aogiri Ridge, 113
Arawe, 112
Ardennes, 76, 94-96
Arezzo, 56
Argentan, 79, 82
Arles, 67
Armed Services Committee, 147
Armies (numbered):
  First, 80, 85, 88-89, 93
  Third, 86, 88
  Fifth, 1, 51, 53-54, 59, 61, 70
  Fifth (U.S.), 1
  Seventh, 39
  Eighth, 129
  Eighth (U.K.), 39, 43-44, 54, 70-71
  Ninth, 89
Army Field Forces, 31
Army groups (numbered):
  12th, 89
  21st, 94
Arnold, Gen. of the Army H. H., 103
Assam, 114
Attu, 101-4, 153
Australia, 99, 111

176

Austria, 55, 58, 64
AVALANCHE, 52
Avezzano, 65
Aviation in Support of Ground Forces (1942), 23-24
Avignon, 67

B

B-3A, 17
B-10, 17
B-17, 4-7, 11, 17, 40-41, 43-47, 50, 57, 59, 62-63, 68-70, 72-74, 77-78, 82, 84, 88, 92, 101, 105, 108, 123, 150-51
B-24, 4-7, 40-41, 43-44, 47, 50, 55, 57, 59, 62-63, 68-70, 72-74, 77-79, 81, 84-85, 87, 101, 103-8, 110-18, 121, 123, 150-52, 154
B-25, 44, 48, 50, 113, 117, 123
B-26, 46, 48, 50, 63, 113, 123, 130, 136
B-29, 2-7, 98, 114, 119-21, 125-48, 151, 153
Badoglio, Marshal, 51
Balikpapan, 110
Baneasa, 69
Bangkok, 116
Barcus, Maj. Gen. Glenn. O., 145
Barcus Board
  See Air Power Evaluation Group.
Battipaglia, 52, 54
BAYTOWN, 39, 52
Beaufighters, 111
Belgium, 88
Bengazi, 41-44
Bering Sea, 101
Betio, 106-7, 154
Biak, 109
Bisley (RAF), 45
Bismarck Archipelago, 99, 112
Bismarck Sea, 111
Bizerte, 48
"Black Cats", 108

Bologna, 51, 70-72, 97, 152
Bombardment Aviation (1931), 16
Bomber Command (RAF), 74, 77, 80-81, 89
Borneo, 98, 109-11
Bougainville, 109
Bradley, Gen. Omar N., 7
Brereton, Maj. Gen. Lewis H., 41, 114
Brereton Detachment, 41
Brisbane, 111
Bucharest, 69
Bulge, Battle of the, 95-96
Burma, 98, 114-16, 118, 146, 152
Butler, Brig. Gen. William O., 100

C

Caen, 76, 78-83, 96-97, 154
Calcutta, 114
Campoleone, 58
Canton, 118
Cape Gloucester, 112, 152
Caroline Is., 99, 109
Casablanca, 42
Cassino, 29, 51, 60-63, 72, 144, 152
Castelnuovo, 53
Central Pacific Area Command, 99, 104-6, 110
Changjon, 136
Changsha, 118
Chengtu, 114
Chennault, Brig. Gen. Claire L., 117
Cherbourg, 77, 80, 83
Chichagof, 101
China, 41, 98-99, 114, 116-19, 121, 124
China Air Task Force, 117
China-Burma-India theater, 41, 100, 113-22
Chinnampo, 128, 131, 138
Chongjin, 131, 136
Chorwon, 137
Chungking, 118, 121
Ciampino, 57
Civitavecchia, 56

AHS-88, Index

Clark, Gen. Mark, 60
Coblenz, 89, 95
COBRA, 83-84
Cold Bay, 100
Cologne, 95
Combined Bomber Offensive, 11, 51,
   55, 57, 64, 68, 70, 74, 150
Combined Chiefs of Staff, 74
Command and Employment of Air
   Power (1943), 27-30
Commands (numbered):
   IX Bomber, 41, 50, 81, 85
   IX Fighter, 79
   IX Tactical Air, 89
   XII Air Support, 45, 52
   XII Bomber, 43, 45, 55
   XII Fighter, 42
   XIII Bomber, 109-10, 122
   XX Bomber, 114, 119-20
   XXI Bomber, 119-20
   XXIX Tactical Air, 89
Congress, 11, 147
Coningham, AM Sir Arthur, 46
CORKSCREW, 49, 51-52
Corps (numbered):
   I, 136
   II, 45
   V, 80
   VI (Fifth Army), 1, 60
   VII (First Army), 88-89
   X, 137
   XX, 86
Corregidor, 110
Coutances, 79
Crete, 45, 47
CROSSBOW, 73, 77, 150
Curtiss Condor, 17

D

Darwin, 111
Del Monte, 110
Desert Air Force (RAF), 52
DH-4, 1
DIADEM, 51, 64-66
Director of Bombardment, 26, 47

Divisions (numbered):
   1st Bomb., 84, 87, 92
   1st Cav., 133, 136
   2d Bomb., 87, 92-94
   3d Bomb., 88, 92-93
   5th Inf., 88
   30th Inf., 7, 90
   32d Inf., 103
   104th Inf., 94
Doolittle, Maj. Gen. James H., 42,
   55, 119
DRAGOON, 39, 66-69
Düren, 89
Dutch Harbor, 100

E

Eaker, Lt. Gen. Ira C., 56-57, 61-62
Eastern Air Command, 116
Eboli, 52-54
Egypt, 24, 41-43
Eisenhower, Gen. of the Army Dwight
   D., 7, 74-75
El Alamein, 40, 43-44
Ellice Is., 99, 105
Empoli, 56
Eniwetok, 109
Eschweiler, 76, 88-94, 96, 153
Espiritu Santo, 108

F

F-84, 140
F-86, 140
Faid Pass, 45
Falconara, 56
Far East Air Forces, 105, 109, 111,
   126, 128-31, 133-34, 139-41;
   Bomber Command, 2, 126, 128-32,
   134-37, 139-41, 143-44;
   Evaluation Division, 138;
   Operations Order No. 204-21,
   141-42
Far East Command, 128
FE-2B, 1
Field Manual 1-5 (1940), 20

Field Manual 31-35, 23-25, 38
Field Manual 100-20, 9, 27-30, 35, 43, 47, 151
Fiji Is., 99
Finschhafen, 112
Florence, 56-57
Foggia, 52, 55
Foligno, 56
Foreign Relations Committee, 147
Formosa, 118, 120
France, 20, 39, 57-58, 64, 66-69, 73-74, 77, 152, 154
Free French, 45
Funafuti Is., 105

G

Gadames, 45-47
Gaya, 114
Geilenkirchen, 89
General Staff, 14, 19, 28, 34
Genoa, 64, 67
Gerbini airfields, 50
German Air Force, 44, 56-58, 69
Germany, 10-11, 55, 64, 73, 150
Ghormley, Vice Adm. Robert L., 100
GHQ Air Force, 15, 17-18, 20, 33. See also Air Force Combat Command
GHQ Target Analysis Group, 129
Gilbert Is., 99, 105-6
Gizo, 108, 110
Gold Beach, 77
Gothic Line, 64
Groups:
  1st Prov. Bomb., 41
  3d Bomb., 136
  5th Bomb., 108, 110
  7th Bomb., 114-15, 117
  11th Bomb., 108
  19th Bomb., 125, 127, 141-42
  22d Bomb., 126, 128, 136, 144
  43d Bomb., 113
  90th Bomb., 113
  92d Bomb., 126, 128, 136, 144
  98th Bomb., 41, 126
  205 (RAF), 64
  307th Bomb., 110, 126
  380th Bomb., 113

Guadalcanal, 99, 108-9
Guam, 105, 119, 125
Gura, Eritrea, 40
Gustav Line, 59-61

H

Haeju, 131
Hainan, 117
Hale, Maj. Gen. Willis H., 104
Halsey, Vice Adm. William F., 100
Halverson, Col. Harry A., 43
Halverson Detachment, 41
Hamhung, 131, 138
Handley-Page, 1
Hankow, 118
Harmon, Maj. Gen. Millard F., 108
Harris, Marshal of the RAF Sir Arthur T., 7
Hawaiian Is., 99, 104
Henderson Field, 109
Hitler, Adolf, 58
Hoeryong, 136
Hokkaido, 104
Hollandia, 111
Hong Kong, 111
Hsian, 118
Hump, 114, 116-17
Hungnam, 131, 135, 138-39, 143
HUSKY, 49-52
Hwangju, 138

I

Inchon, 125
Independent Force, 10, 33
India, 98, 114
Insein, 115
Italian Air Force, 44
Italy, 4, 37, 39-40, 42, 47, 49-66, 70-72, 73-74, 96, 146, 150-52
Itazuke, 142
Iwo Jima, 119-20, 151

J

Japan, 98, 111, 119-20, 150
Japanese Air Force, 100, 106, 116
Java, 111

Joint Chiefs of Staff, 55, 132
Joint Operations Center, 132
Joint Training Directive for Air-Ground Operations, 31-32
Julich, 89
Juno Beach, 77

K

Kaesong, 125
Kanni, 135
Kasserine Pass, 29, 40, 43, 45-47
Kenney, Maj. Gen. George C., 111
Kesselring, FM Albert, 58, 70-72
Keystone Panther, 17
Kimpo airfield, 127
Kinkaid, Vice Adm. Thomas C., 99, 102
Kiska, 100-101, 104
Kluge, FM Günther von, 82
Knightsbridge, 24, 41
Kobe, 119
Korea, 124-48, 150-51, 153
Kosong, 130
Kowon, 142-43
Kunming, 117
Kurils, 104, 119
Kuter, Brig. Gen. Laurence S., 45-46
Kwajalein, 105, 109
Kyushu, 119-20, 151

L

Lae, 112
Langerwehe, 89, 92-93
Langley Field, 14
Leigh-Mallory, ACM Sir Trafford, 74, 83-84
Leyte, 109
Liberators (RAF), 116
Libya, 43, 45, 49
Lingayen Gulf, 109-10
Lisieux, 79
Los Negros, 109
Low Countries, 20, 73
Luxembourg, 86
Luzon, 105, 122
Lynd, Brig. Gen. William E., 102
Lyons, 67

M

MacArthur, Gen. Douglas, 99, 111, 134, 144
McKinnon, Col. Morton H., 27
McNair, Lt. Gen. Lesley J., 7, 85
MADISON, 86
Mainz, 95
Malta, 49
Manchuria, 121, 125, 135-36, 139
Mandalay, 114
Manus I., 112
Mareth Line, 44-45
Mariana Is., 99, 119-20
Marine Corps, 106-7, 113
Marquesas Is., 99
Marseilles, 67
Marshall Is., 99, 105
Mediterranean Air Command, 43
Mediterranean Allied Air Forces, 56-57, 59, 65-66
Mediterranean Allied Strategic Air Force, 56-58, 64, 66-70
Mediterranean Allied Tactical Air Force, 56-58, 61-62, 64, 70
Messerschmitt plants, 56
Messina, 42, 50-51
Metz, 76, 86-88, 94, 96, 153
Meuse R., 94
Middle East Review (RAF), 44, 46
Midway, 105
MIG-15, 140, 153
Mignano, 53
Milan, 64
Mindanao, 110
Mindoro, 109
Mingaladon, 115
Mitchell, Brig. Gen. William, 10
Mitsubishi, 105
Mokpo, 142
Monte Cassino, 60-61
Montgomery, FM Bernard L., 30, 44
Morocco, 42
Moselle R., 86
Moulmein, 115
Munda air base, 109
Muzon, 110

N

Nagoya, 119
Naktong R., 133

Namgong-ni, 135
Naples, 42, 55
Navy, 102-3, 106, 108, 123
Nemi, 65
New Britain, 111-12
New Caledonia, 99
New Delhi, 114
New Georgia, 109
New Guinea, 99, 109
New Hebrides Is., 99, 108
New Zealand, 99
Nimitz, Adm. Chester W., 99, 102, 109
Noemfoor, 109, 111-12
Normandy, 66, 73-74, 76-79, 81-83, 86, 96, 149-50, 152, 154
North Pacific Area Command, 99, 100-104
North Sea, 91
Northwest African Air Forces, 25, 43, 49
Northwest African Strategic Air Force, 43, 46, 50, 52-54
Northwest African Tactical Air Force, 25, 43, 46, 49-50, 52-53

O

O'Donnell, Maj. Gen. Emmett, Jr., 132-33, 135, 146-47
Okinawa, 105, 110-11, 120, 125, 142
Omaha Beach, 77, 80
Onjong-ni, 138, 142-43
Osaka, 119
Otopeni airdrome, 69

P

P-38, 50, 103
P-39, 45
P-40, 44-45
P-51H, 5
Pacific Ocean Areas, 99
Padua, 64
Palau Is., 105
Palawan, 110
Palermo, 42
Palestine, 42
Palestrina, 65
Pandaveswar, 114

Pantelleria, 39, 49, 61
Paramushiru, 104
Patton, Gen. George, 82, 86, 94
PB4Y, 108
Pearl Harbor, 100, 105
Peenemünde, 75
Périers, 83
Perugia, 57
Philippine Is., 99, 105, 111, 118
Phoenix Is., 99
Picardy, 1, 3
Pisa, 52, 56-57
Pistoia, 56
Ploesti, 41, 50
Po R., 70-71
Poland, 19-20
Pompei, 53
Prato, 56
Pusan, 124, 128, 131-32
Pyongyang, 130-31, 136, 139, 141-43

R

Rabaul, 109
Radio and radar:
  AN-APN-3, 148
  AN-MPQ-2, 136, 138-39, 142, 145-48
  Gee-H, 87-88, 92
  H2X, 78-79, 87-88, 91-92
  Micro-H, 92
  SCS-51, 87, 91-92
Rangoon, 114-16, 121
Rashin, 131, 139
Razorback Hill, 113
Regensburg-Prüfening, 56
Reggio, 39
Reketa Bay, 108, 110
Rhine R., 95
Rhône R., 67
Richardson, Lt. Gen. Robert C., 106
Rimini, 56, 64
Rising Sun Refinery, 127
Roer R., 89, 92
Rome, 50, 54-55, 57, 59
Rommell, Marshal, 25, 44-46, 48
Royal Air Force, 10, 24, 33, 41-44, 49, 73, 82, 92-93, 115-16, 122
Royal Australian Air Force, 111
Royal Navy, 1, 81
Rumania, 39, 51, 69
Russell, Senator Richard B., 147

S

Saar, 86
Saarbrücken, 87-88
Saarlautern, 87
Saint-Lô, 7, 76, 83-86, 91, 96-97, 152, 154
Saipan, 105, 109, 119
Salerno, 29, 51-55, 66, 72, 80, 97, 152
Salween R., 118
Samoa Is., 99
San Jose, 110
San Vicente, 110
Sarana valley, 103
Sardinia, 49-50
Sariwon, 130
Savona, 67
SBD, 123
Second Army (British), 81
2d Battalion, 32d Inf. Div., 103
Seine Bay, 81
Seoul, 125, 127, 137-38, 142
Sète, 67
Shafroth, Rear Adm. John F., 99
Shanghai, 105
Shaw, Capt. Norman, 146
Shimushu, 104
SHINGLE, 55
Sicily, 39, 42, 49-50, 66
Siena, 56
Sinanju, 139
Sinchon, 136, 145
Singosan, 142
Simuiju, 136
"Snooper Squadron", 108
Solomon Is., 99, 108
Songchon, 139
Songjin, 131, 135
South Pacific Area Command, 99, 108-10
South Pole, 99
Southeast Pacific Area, 99
Southwest Pacific Area, 99, 108-13
Spaatz, Lt. Gen. Carl, 43, 47, 74
Squadrons (numbered):
  36th Bombardment, 101
  91st Strategic Reconnaissance, 142
  160 (RAF), 41
  308th Bombardment, 115
  345th Bombardment, 146

Strait of Messina, 50, 52
STRANGLE (World War II), 37-38, 64-65, 72, 150
Strategic Air Force (CBI), 116
Stratemeyer, Lt. Gen. George E., 115-16, 130-31
Subiaco, 65
Suez Canal, 46
Sunchen, 139
Supreme Headquarters, Allied Expeditionary Forces, 74-76
Sword Beach, 77

T

Tactical Air Command, 31
Tactical Air Control Center, 144
Taegu, 124
Tanchon, 136
Tanyang, 128
Tarawa, 105-7, 154
TBF, 123
Tedder, ACM Sir Arthur W., 43, 76
Terni, 58
The Air Force (1931), 14, 20
The Air Force in Theaters of Operation Organization and Functions (1943), 26
The Employment of the Air Forces of the Army (1935), 17, 33
Theobald, Rear Adm. Robert A., 99-100
Thionville, 76, 86-88, 94, 96, 153
Tientsin, 114
Tinian, 119
Tobruk, 24, 41, 44-45
Tokyo, 40, 119
TORCH, 42
Torre Annunziata, 53
Torre del Greco, 53
Toulon, 39, 66-68
Training Circular 70 (1941), 22-23, 34, 35
Training Directive 52 (1941), 20-22
Training Regulation 440-15 (1926), 35; (1935), 18-20, 33, 35
Truk, 105, 109
Tuamotu Archipelago, 99
Tunisia, 42-45, 55
Turin, 56, 64
Twining, Brig. Gen. Nathan F., 108

U

Umnak, 100
United Kingdom, 36, 73-74, 151
United Nations, 2, 124-26
United Soviet Socialist Republics, 39
United States Army Middle East Air Force, 41-42, 44
United States Strategic Air Forces in Europe, 74
United States Strategic Bombing Survey, 11, 36-37, 106, 149
Utah Beach, 79

V

Valence, 67
Vardenberg, Gen. Hoyt S., 140
Venafro, 62
Verona, 64
Villarotunda, 62
Voghera, 56

W

Waegwan, 132-34, 147, 154
War Department, 14, 17, 20
Wellington (RAF), 1-2, 40, 43-44
Western Desert Air Force (RAF), 41
Weyland, Lt. Gen. Otto P., 140, 145
Williamson, Col. Charles G., 26
Wilson, Gen. Sir Henry M., 57, 60-61, 66
Wings (numbered):
  19th Bombardment, 138
  98th Bombardment, 142
Woleai, 109
Wonsan, 127, 130-31
WOWSER, 71

Y

Yangtze River, 118
Yap, 109
Yenangyung, 116
Yokota, 126
YOKUM, 68
Yonghung, 139
Yosu, 141-42
Yunnan, 117

www.ingramcontent.com/pod-product-compliance
Lightning Source LLC
Chambersburg PA
CBHW082121230426
43671CB00015B/2761